I Love My Amma

Praise for *I Love My Amma*

'The book by celebrated Kannada writer Vasudhendra is a collection of memoir essays about his mother. In most of them, the mother herself is the central character. Merely offering a portrait of her, the essays also allow us to grasp her outlook on life. In some pieces, while the writer recalls other memories, the mother briefly appears with her own distinct presence. In the essay about drinking, her role is small, yet it shines like a gemstone, illuminating the entire piece.

'The book can also be read as an autobiographical work as it reveals his parents, his hometown and the background he comes from. Flashes of humour and self-mockery scattered throughout make the reader laugh aloud. At the same time, moments shadowed by sorrow run quietly beneath the surface. Once you finish one essay, it is hard to resist moving immediately to the next. It is a book that compels you to read it in a single sitting.

'Because the book is about a mother, it made me reflect on my own mother and her surprising similarities with Vasudhendra's, despite their different backgrounds. For instance, the obsession mothers often have with utensils—I have written an essay about this myself, and Vasudhendra has written one as well.'

– Perumal Murugan

'The spontaneity, wit, wisdom and heart-rending humour of these quotidian tales and loving recollections about Vasudhendra's Amma carry the universality of all great art.'

– Namita Gokhale

I Love My Amma

VASUDHENDRA

TRANSLATED *from* THE KANNADA *by*
Narayan Shankaran

HARPER
NON-FICTION

First published in India by Harper Non-Fiction 2026
An imprint of HarperCollins *Publishers*
HarperCollins *Publishers India*, Cyber City,
Building 10-A, Gurugram, Haryana – 122002, India
www.harpercollins.co.in

2 4 6 8 10 9 7 5 3 1

P-ISBN: 978-93-7307-104-6
E-ISBN: 978-93-7307-314-9

Typeset in 11/14 Adobe Caslon Pro
by HarperCollins *Publishers* India Pvt. Ltd

Printed and bound at
Nutech Print Services Pvt. Ltd.

FSC
www.fsc.org
MIX
Paper | Supporting responsible forestry
FSC® C195953

This book is printed on FSC® certified paper
which ensures responsible forest management.

HarperCollins *Publishers*, Macken House, 39/40 Mayor Street Upper, Dublin 1, D01 C9W8, Ireland

CONTENTS

INTRODUCTION

Amma and My Pension

EVEN THE MOST SKILLED STORYTELLERS FACE difficulty when they set out to write their autobiography. That fine line between imagination and truth tends to get blurred in their minds. At some point, they almost start believing the stories so beautifully woven by their imagination to be true. This very imagination, which helps them spin yarn after yarn, is both their strength and their weakness. Without it, they cannot write vivid and juicy stories. But thanks to their excellent craft, when authors unveil seemingly bizarre anecdotes in their autobiographical works, readers begin to wonder if all those incidents could have actually happened at all!

While I can't speak for others, as far as this memoir, *I Love My Amma*, is concerned, I can say that all events I have described here are based on true incidents—albeit with some embellishments. In fact, that's the reason why I have consciously refrained from mentioning my parents' names in any of the essays. Moreover, in order to keep it simple, I have merged my two elder sisters into one, and portrayed just one older sister. However, the incidents involving my older sister in the book are based on things my two older sisters actually did. I have deliberately avoided revealing my name as well. I leave it to my readers to decide whether to read this book as an autobiographical creation or a work of fiction.

As long as Amma was alive, it never occurred to me to write about her. But after she passed away, I wrote about her incessantly. For a couple of months after her death, I was devastated by the onslaught of memories that involved her. It was only then that I realized how deeply she had pervaded my entire being. Writing these essays seemed to have a therapeutic effect and helped me cope with the intense grief I felt after losing her. But writing about her again and again turned into an addiction of sorts. So much so, I struggled to write about anything else for a long time. Even now, I have a host of stories about her lurking within—Amma is an unlimited source of stories. But with the passage of time, as I came to terms with her passing, I found that I couldn't go on writing about her. Moreover, it gets monotonous for a writer to write about the same thing over and over again. I felt similarly when I found myself writing story after story about queer people after I wrote *Mohanaswamy*.

Amma had a colourful personality. Whatever she did, she did with great intensity—whether it was performing rigorous religious rituals; cooking for a hundred guests; shouldering the entire responsibility of a wedding celebration; raising a debt while in dire straits; nursing the sick; or engaging in a street quarrel, regardless of the opponent being a man or a woman. She lived a forthright, unconcealed life. She had been raised with no notion of the so-called urban modesty.

If she was at a wedding, a crowd would always gather around her and eagerly listen to her words.

She also loved with the same intensity with which she did everything else. At times, I couldn't bear how possessive she was of me. She found it hard to tolerate anyone else entering my world. As her only son, I often felt caught in a vice-like grip of intense love. I was so surrounded by her protective care that I hardly had any sense of individuality left. She would leave no stone unturned to make sure of my safety and well-being. While I'd get angry when her love turned proprietary and threatened my personal freedom, at other times, I'd find myself melting in the warm embrace of knowing how much love she had for me. After her demise, I wrote these essays by consciously distancing myself from her, to the extent that I could. The fact that she would never get to read them gave me the courage to write about her honestly, I guess.

I Love My Amma happened quite unexpectedly. One day, a couple of months after she passed away, while I was shaving, I looked into my own eyes in the mirror and suddenly felt that I was looking into Amma's eyes. Then it occurred to me that the bowel problems she suffered in her final days were very similar to the problems I had faced in my childhood. That realization made me feel as though Amma and I were suddenly one. In that moment, I felt as though she had not really died but was very much alive within me. That very day, I sat down and wrote the entire essay. While I had written a few stories by then, I was not very sure how to write an essay. So, I decided to play to my strengths. By using time shifting technique where characters swap places, I wrote the essay as if it were a story. Incidentally, a few days later a major Kannada daily called for entries for a short story competition. Though I wasn't sure if I had written a story or an essay, I sent in my entry anyway. But the jury rejected it outright. I later came to know that the judges had apparently said that it was just an attempt at emotional blackmail, and that the piece could not be considered as a story at all. Although I was a little disappointed with the remarks of the jury, I took it in stride and moved on. But I did wonder if anybody would want to read essays peppered with personal experiences.

Then, something unexpected occurred. Though the story was not considered for the competition, its emotional intensity had impressed the editor of the daily. He published it in two instalments in his newspaper. Fortunately, the story was very well received by Kannada readers. In those days, in the absence of social media, it was customary to include the writer's contact details along with published stories. Calls and letters poured in like never before. I was quite overwhelmed by the responses from readers. Some could relate to similar incidents that had happened in their own homes. Some talked about how hard they had struggled to openly speak about such incidents. Some youngsters sincerely admitted that this story changed the way they looked at their mothers. These reactions felt special to me and bolstered up my confidence greatly. In my mother's story, many could find reflections of their own. Many could see their wives, sisters or grandmothers in Amma. Thankfully, without having to write a preachy book titled *How to Love Your Mother*, through this simple essay, I had helped my readers tap into the boundless love they felt for their mothers. Initially, I was wary of publishing such a personal essay and feared readers' rejection. But when I saw the positive responses, I realized that although many had undergone similar experiences, few had dared to narrate them with compassion and courage. Slowly, I came to realize that my candid and uninhibited narration of personal experiences was the main reason readers appreciated my essays. In our society, many topics that are regarded as taboo remain unspoken due to false notions of respectability. Once someone dares to go against the grain and boldly writes about such stigmatized topics, more voices tend to join in.

After the Kannada version of the essay 'I Love My Amma' became popular among readers, editors started requesting essays about my mother more frequently. Year after year, for Mother's Day or Women's Day, I would receive requests for such pieces from almost all major newspapers. As if in response to the demand, many stories connected with Amma began to naturally flow out of me. As I kept writing, the praise for my essays poured in. Beyond supportive publishers and appreciative readers, what more can a writer ask for? So I kept on writing. Besides unveiling my mother's personality, these stories included many anecdotes of our townspeople and their lifestyles, and glimpses into my childhood as well. I gradually understood that these stories were not just mine but belonged to many others too.

Readers across demographics have often told me that the childhood described in these essays belonged to them as well. The universality of these essays ensured that they were soon translated into Tamil, Telugu and Konkani. Cutting across linguistic barriers, even those living thousands of kilometres away from the small town I grew up in, in Bellary, could relate to my essays as if they were their own. If there is anything called 'Indianness', perhaps it manifests most profoundly in this shared divine experience.

Frankly speaking, I loved and respected my father a shade more than I did my mother. He was a harmless man, who'd never hurt anyone. He was so taciturn that quarrelling or arguing was beyond him. All through his life, he silently toiled on to protect his family—never once cribbing or complaining. Forget raising his hand to thrash me, he hardly ever yelled at me even when he was angry.

Despite having such contrasting natures, my parents had a harmonious marriage. I have seldom seen them quarrel. My father had quietly surrendered to my mother's towering personality, and had found peace in that acceptance. He never had to regret it because Amma never took advantage of his timidity. Despite being the head of our household, Amma never treated Appa disrespectfully. In his final days, Appa lost control over his right arm and couldn't wear his dhoti or shirt on his own. Amma patiently took care of all these tasks for him.

Appa passed away a year before Amma did. Strangely, Appa's loss did not affect me emotionally. Forget writing an engaging story, I didn't even write a few lines about him. Compared to my mother's colourful personality, my father seemed plain and sombre. Exceptionally good people hardly make a good subject for compelling stories.

Amma never got over the pain of losing Appa. In deep depression, she barely managed to hold up for about a year before she passed away. Both died without getting bedridden or hospitalized. Just like the clicks of a camera shutter, their lives ended instantaneously—without much suffering.

Amma had mastered the art of storytelling. She enjoyed reading weeklies, monthlies and novels, and hardly missed any film that came to town. After dinner, she would often narrate them to us as bedtime stories. Seated around her, my sisters and I would listen to her with our eyes wide and our mouths open. Even my father would join us in these story sessions. In our hot hometown, it was customary for us to sleep in the courtyard in the summers. So, in those midsummer nights, Amma's audience grew as our neighbours also joined us to listen to her tales. A larger audience would egg her on further.

Her charged-up narratives didn't have any room for hesitation or restraint. The films of that time often contained scenes of rape and molestation, and Amma had no qualms about openly describing such scenes with expressions like, 'The bastard raped the girl, made her pregnant, and left her high and dry.'

She not only told stories that she'd read but also created anecdotes from her own experiences, and narrated them in a delightful way. With her impeccable oratory skills, she would stretch a mere one-day trip to nearby Bellary city into a week-long saga. I'd often notice that she'd add quite a few white lies to spice up her stories. But her lies were always so harmless and charming that no one ever objected. With a straight face, she often spoke of seeing numerous ghosts. It wasn't uncommon for her to argue and interact with ghosts and spirits in her anecdotes. She spoke with such conviction that we naively believed her. Although many of our elders never wrote stories, their oral storytelling had more power than our written words.

Writers are most influenced by their childhood. I've noticed that a few writers have been happy writing only about their childhoods all their lives. Perhaps, experiences and impressions from our childhood remain so vividly etched in our memories because, as children, we see life without any prejudice. Elders often bid children to sit quietly and observe everything. 'Keep silent' is the most common command children hear in their growing-up years. Staying silent sharpens the power of perception in children. But as soon as we grow up and start earning money, we somehow forget the art of listening and observation. Suddenly, we fancy ourselves as know-alls and develop various kinds of biases. In the process, we quite unwittingly lose the respect and awe we had for our elders in our childhood. Perhaps, that is why authors struggle to write about their later years with the same ease and depth with which they depict their childhood. In our youth, our parents no longer appear as the vibrant heroes they once were in our childhood. But if we confine our writing entirely to childhood, our work becomes clichéd. A storyteller's greatest challenge is to retain the wonder and innocence of childhood, even while speaking in a mature and wise voice that time teaches us.

Kannada literature has embraced the tradition of writing essays sprinkled with personal anecdotes. This genre is known as 'Lalita Prabandhagalu', meaning informal or light essays. Although such essays are usually about the author's own experiences, they are not always limited to them. Sometimes, when a friend's experiences seamlessly blend in with the subject of the essay, the author may take the liberty of incorporating them as his own. As these essays are usually in first-person narrative, they evoke a vivid and lively experience in readers. While there's some room for imagination, it cannot overstep reality. They encompass a touch of humour, a bit of sentiment, the subtle nuances of human relationships, and a shot of despair and distress. Unlike short stories, these essays do not demand a strict structure—they are free from the constraints of a clear beginning, middle or end. Just as maize plants happily sway when a breeze blows across the open plains, these essays too can freely meander unchecked. Veteran writers like Kuvempu, Pu.Ti. Narasimhachar and A.N. Murthy Rao have made significant contributions to this genre.

The Kannada original of this book, *Nammamma Andre Nangishta*, has been hugely popular among readers and has sold over 30,000 copies so far. It has received several awards, including the Karnataka Sahitya Academy's book award. Not all Kannada books sell in such large numbers. In addition to reader appreciation, several other factors have contributed to the distinction this book has achieved. Many literature-loving Kannadigas follow the tradition of giving a literary work as a return gift to guests on special occasions like weddings, thread ceremonies, housewarmings, etc. Since this small book is perfectly suited for such gifting, people have often bought this book in bulk. Many have distributed this book as a memento during the Vaikunta Samaradhane ceremony of their beloved parents or elders. As I am the publisher of all my books, customers make these bulk purchases directly from me at a reasonable price.

Over the years, several essays from *Nammamma Andre Nangishtha* have caught the imagination of theatre enthusiasts. Many amateur drama troupes have adapted individual essays into plays and presented them on stage to great success. A play based on the essay about my mother's obsession with stainless steel utensils has had over fifty performances at

Ranga Shankara, and is still staged occasionally. Theatre professionals often tell me that my stories, novels and essays are easily adaptable for the stage and for films. Once, the renowned Kannada actor-director Ramesh Aravind expressed his wish to make a film by combining all the essays found in this book. He wanted to act in it and direct it himself, and wished to dedicate the movie to his mother on her seventy-fifth birthday. I even wrote the screenplay for him, which he liked very much. However, producers in the Kannada film industry felt that a film about an elderly woman wouldn't attract the masses to movie halls, and didn't dare to invest in the movie. Consequently, the project had to be shelved.

One essay from this collection is included as a lesson in the Kannada textbook in the ICSE curriculum. Many Kannada-medium schools have adopted this work as an optional text. Many schools give this book as a prize to the winners of various competitions. Over the years, on many occasions, several schools have invited me to speak to their students. Such interactions bring me great joy. From the elderly right up to schoolchildren, people of all ages have read my work. In fact, I have never felt the need to write anything exclusively for any particular age group.

In some schools, students are often given the assignment to interview me or collect information about me. Sometimes, they visit my home for these interviews. Such encounters are always both enjoyable and challenging. When they see hundreds of books stacked on the bookshelves, they curiously ask me, 'Have you read all these books?' I smile and honestly admit that I haven't. Then they ask, 'So why do you keep buying them?' and I find it hard to explain how obsessed a book lover is in acquiring books.

As a publisher, I have adopted a strategy of selling this book at a very reasonable price. For many years, we offered *Nammamma Andre Nangishtha* as the 'student edition', for about ₹65–70. Presently, the Kannada edition costs ₹100. The affordability of this book is another reason for its popularity. My experience is that once readers finish this book, they inevitably buy my other works as well. As a vendor of sweets uses free samples to lure his customers into buying more of his sweets, I have successfully used this book to market my other books. Even today, when I meet my readers at book fairs and literature fests, many of them tell me that this was the first book of mine they read, and then went on to buy and read all the others. Since this book has gone through many reprints, I have commissioned different artists to create a variety of covers. Some ardent fans have purchased all the editions with different covers for their collection.

However, my mother was very annoyed and resented me in one particular matter. As I was a bright student, by the time I completed engineering, I had received several placement offers from many MNCs as well as from premier central government institutions like Indian Space Research Organization (ISRO) and Defence Research and Development Organization (DRDO). In those days, everyone in my peer group preferred to work for private companies, and regarded joining the government service as old school. We had a strong conviction that our personal growth would be much greater in the private sector. So, much against Amma's wishes, I joined a private company. She was obviously offended by my choice and couldn't comprehend my obstinate behaviour. She angrily asked, 'Do you really want to forgo a government job that fetches you a lifelong pension even after retirement and join a private company? Have you gone mad, or what?' Having slowly cultivated some defiance, much against her wishes, I went on to join a private firm. Even after learning that I was earning a good salary, she never stopped asking, 'What will happen to you after you retire? Who will take care of your expenses in your old age?'

I would simply smile at her and brush away her persistent concern. Now, after she's gone, I sometimes wonder if this book, with its ever-soaring sales, has turned out to be the source of my pension! I sometimes fancifully imagine that she might have made me write this book only to make sure that I got the pension I missed by not joining the government service, and laugh at my own thoughts.

I live almost like an atheist. Forget observing any religious rituals, I don't even wear a janivara on my shoulder. On the other hand, both my father and mother lived a deeply traditional and devout life in strict compliance with their faith until their last days. The fact that I don't perform the annual shraddha to either of them greatly pains my two elder sisters. They often quarrel with me about my apathy and indifference to religious rites and rituals. Whenever I face any difficulty in life, my sisters say that our parents are troubling me because they are very angry with me for not performing their shraddha. Since I have no desire to change my ways and start performing these rites, I try to comfort them with a reassuring thought, by saying, 'Shraddha is nothing but remembering one's elders with devotion. Each day, there is a reader reading this book somewhere. While doing so, I'm sure they remember our parents with respect. Therefore, through this book, I am performing shraddha for my parents every day.' Although my sisters are far from convinced by my explanation, they have certainly reduced their cribbing.

Now that this work is reaching the hands of English readers, I am truly delighted. I take this opportunity to express my gratitude to the translator, Dr Narayan Shankaran, for his exemplary work. With deep affection I remember my two sisters, Vinoda and Vanaja, who have lovingly cared for me all my life and filled my mother's place since her demise.

12 October 2025 Vasudhendra

1

THE CHADDI RASCAL

19 December 2004

I ADMIT IT WITHOUT EMBARRASSMENT: I WAS A chaddi rascal in my childhood. Although every morning, Appa and Amma repeatedly yelled at me for not going to the toilet, I would say 'not coming…' and dodge going to the loo for almost a couple of days on the trot. I hated the filthy stench of the toilet. Rather than yelling at me all the time and asking me to go to the toilet, I wished my parents would ask me to go to the nearby candy shop instead. I would have happily gone there, even multiple times. 'You won't get your meal till you go to the paikhana,' Amma would shout reproachfully. Since I somehow managed to hoodwink Appa–Amma and silence them, they couldn't heckle me beyond a point.

Though I could zip up my parents' lips with my tricks, zipping up my own bottom wasn't as easy. After all, my gut is no black hole that would suck in everything I kept gulping down incessantly. It would always act up at the most inconvenient time—making its move, more often than not, right in the middle of school hours. Our Bellary District School didn't have any toilets. Forget a toilet, it didn't even have any water to drink. So, expecting water for a student to take a dump would be too greedy. Although there were a lot of vacant fields around the school, the Headmaster had secured the school premises with a strong fence to prevent students from escaping. I was too scared of my teachers to confide in them about my 'urge'. And what's the use of sharing such a problem with classmates?

I was in Class One back then. Just as our class teacher, Bandri Master, was animatedly teaching us 'Come, come, parrot … coloured parrot', I suddenly felt the pressure coming too! How could a teacher so engrossed in singing understand my predicament?

Swinging himself passionately, he went on, 'Come, come, parrot … coloured parrot.'

'Come, come, parrot … coloured parrot,' all the kids echoed back in unison.

Clenching my teeth and pressing my stomach hard, I tried to shove back the unsolicited guest who was trying to gatecrash. 'No, no, don't come … not now,' I silently kept chanting, like a mantra.

Meanwhile, 'Come, come, parrot …' the teacher screamed again, vehemently.

My control finally gave away. I had goosebumps as I felt a certain warmth at my bottom. My stomach, however, felt pacified after the ease-out. I looked at the kids sitting on either side.

Unaware of the bomb blast amid them, 'Come, come, parrot …' the class kept parroting the teacher. Clearly, the sound of the explosion had died down in the noise.

'Will give you fruit … come, come, come …' the teacher finally moved on to the next line.

But even without the lure of the fruit, the goldie-birdie had already arrived!

Tender nostrils cannot be deceived for long. Boys sitting around could eventually smell the 'crime' and started looking for the culprit. I knew that I'd be caught if I stayed aloof. So, I also closed my nose and started to look around at others, feigning suspicion. I must have done a bit of overacting due to the guilt I carried, for the boys grew suspicious and started fixing their gaze on me. In all the distraction of tracking down the offender, our singing went a little awry, and that caught the attention of Bandri Master.

As all the eyes were fixed on me, the master looked straight at me and said, 'Come on, putta, stand up and recite the rhyme once.'

My frail legs started shaking. I pretended as though I didn't hear a thing.

'You heard me loud and clear, didn't you?' asked the master, picking up his cane.

With no other go, I stood up. As coins trickle out of a torn pocket of trousers, bits of turd fell out of my chaddi. All the boys moved away as though they had stepped on a snake. Bandri Master walked towards me with the cane in his hand. He quickly understood what had happened and covered his nose.

He walked up to me, pinched my ear and snapped, 'Yuck! What did you guzzle up yesterday to stink so fetidly, you idiot? Don't you know that you should ease yourself before coming to school?'

I started bawling loudly. My sister was summoned from Class Four. On account of the Gouri festival, Akka was wearing a new silk frock with a contrast blouse that day.

Adorned with a glowing chain around her neck and jhumkas in her ears, like a putta Gouri, Akka walked in with the ghal-ghal sound of her tinkling anklets. For someone who'd come with the anticipation of getting an invite to sing a song for the evening aarti at Bandri Master's house, the sight of her little brother caught in a sticky mess came as a real shocker. Stupefied, she just stood there, gaping at me blankly.

'Just wash his bottom and clean the place, putti,' Bandri Master told Akka.

I wondered whether Akka would ever do such things? Especially when she's so exquisitely dressed up?

She said, 'I'll bring our Amma,' and scurried away without even waiting for the master's reply.

Everybody stood waiting for my mother's arrival. Staring at me as though I was a convict, the boys started sniggering. Unable to hold back anymore, I began weeping uncontrollably. Thankfully, soon I could see Amma coming at a distance. With a brass pot on her waist and an old cloth in her hand, she was hurriedly walking towards the school. Akka was trailing behind her. I dreaded that Amma would lambast me for what I had done and started crying louder.

As soon as Amma entered the class, she placed the brass pot on the floor and hugged me tightly. Caressing my cheeks affectionately, she pacified me, saying, 'Don't cry, raja, the sky hasn't fallen ... don't cry.'

Her words of solace aggravated my grief even more. Forgetting that I was in a classroom, I wailed shamelessly. Amma's words and presence gave me immense strength and comfort.

After pacifying me, she cleaned the floor with water. As everyone stared at Amma, I felt humiliated. Wiping the floor with the old cloth she had brought, Amma turned to Bandri Master, folded her hands and said, 'Little child, master … such accidents happen sometimes … please forgive him.' She then tucked the cloth into her saree, lifted the pot in one hand, held my hand with the other and walked me back home.

Once home, she removed all my clothes, gave me a nice bath using a fragrant soap and dressed me up in fresh clothes. She then washed my soiled chaddi and put it out to dry.

Feeling guilty for putting Amma through such hardship and humiliation, my voice choked when I said, 'I will never repeat this again, Amma.'

Touched by my promise, she patted my shoulders and nuzzled my hair as she said, 'My little prince,' and fondly kissed me on my cheek. 'Do you know where you were before you were born?' she asked me, chuckling.

I shook my head.

She put my hand on her belly, made me caress it in a circle and said, 'Right here!' and laughed heartily. 'Crouching inside, you would cheekily pee and do potty in my stomach itself; I've cleaned all your filth right in my stomach, you know?' she said, her eyes twinkling.

'Is it?' I asked, in astonishment.

The next day, I started throwing tantrums and refused to go to school, no matter what. I was scared that all my friends would surely gang up to tease me endlessly.

'You better cut that crap and pack off to school at once … otherwise you'll get two tight slaps on your bum, mind you,' Appa threatened as usual.

Akka refused to walk with me to school and went with some of her friends instead.

Amma then made the rare exception of taking out the sandal oil from the almirah, a luxury otherwise preserved only for Deepavali. She applied it on my body and said, 'Look, how nice you smell! Nobody will make fun of you now. In fact, everyone will come and sit with you because of your sandal oil fragrance. Now, come on, be a good boy, come, let's go to school.'

As all her coaxing and the sugar candies she placed in my hands defused my resolve, I soon found myself walking towards the school with Amma. Having reached the school gate, she released my hand to stroke my hair. Feeling somewhat better and confident, I waved back at Amma and entered the school gate. She stood there watching me till I merged into the herd of kids in uniform.

Eventually, I got accustomed to the habit of going to the toilet every morning. I would somehow endure the foul stench of the paikhana for a few minutes and would be done with it. But despite my reforms, I encountered my misfortune once again when I was in Class Three.

Bandri Master had taken all of us for an excursion to the Gandi Narasimha Swamy Temple once. It's on a beautiful hilly woodland about 6.5 kilometres from our town. All the trekking and playing in the blazing sun had made us quite hungry. So the extra hot and spicy lunch prepared by the local cook didn't deter us from gobbling up a bellyful. I ended up eating a couple of morsels more than I usually do, despite water coming out of my eyes and nose. I felt the effect of my indulgence only in the evening.

Just as the picnic was about to pack up, I felt the 'urge'. I noticed that the brook had dried up as it was summer. I could also not spot a suitable bush or shrub nearby. Just as I was considering taking Bandri Master into confidence, suddenly it reached the threshold. Even before I could realize, history repeated itself! And I'd become a chaddi rascal again!

But this time round, I was quite determined to keep the matter strictly under wraps. No matter what, I didn't want to refresh anyone's memory and reinforce my credentials as a chaddi rascal all over again. Silently, I entered a cave I had come across in the knoll next to the brook and hid myself there. I was too scared of the humiliation I would face if the boys or Bandri Master found out about the matter. Amid all the fun, frolic and hullabaloo of packing up, nobody noticed my absence at all. Soon, all the noise died down as everyone left the place. With everybody gone and dusk setting in, an eerie silence prevailed in the surroundings. When I hesitantly stepped out of the cave, I could see the thrown-away plantain leaves of our lunch flying here and there in the wind. I was scared out of my wits; I didn't know my way home. Not knowing what to do, I sat sobbing in the dark. As it got darker, bats started flying around and monkeys started screeching. The fiercely blowing wind passing through the creeks of the cave produced a sound akin to someone crying hoarse. Petrified, I started chanting 'Ramanama', and kept pacing back and forth for a while. I got tired after some time and eventually dozed off in a corner of the cave.

Probably a couple of hours had passed when I woke up due to the freezing cold. I could hear some familiar voices nearby, so I looked out of the cave and spotted Akka and Amma sitting at a little distance and talking. I could see them clearly because Akka had a lantern in her hand. Crying loudly, I sprinted towards Amma. She hugged me tight and joined me in my crying. Apparently, Amma and Akka had been wandering there shouting 'raja' and 'putta' for quite some time, but I hadn't heard a thing because I had been fast asleep. On the way back home, every now and then Amma kept cursing Bandri Master and the other boys for leaving behind her little prince alone in the forest.

'Why the hell didn't you come along with all the others, you dimwit? Why did you stay back like a fool?' Akka asked me, while wiping her tears with her arm.

I briefed them about the awkward mess I had gotten into.

'Oh my God! This is a forest where leopards and tigers roam around. Why did you hide in the cave as though you'd done something no one has ever done? What if something had gone wrong? My God!' said Amma, folding her hands towards the direction of the Narasimha Swamy Temple's gopura. Akka and I also folded our hands.

After dropping us home, Amma ran down to Bandri Master's house to give him an earful for leaving me behind. The master apologized, 'Sorry, Amma, I missed him in that chaos. I should have been more careful.'

That night, Amma slept next to me and kept patting my back till I fell asleep.

Seeing my plight, the following day Amma bought me some new underwear. So what if it was just an underwear? It's still a new garment, right? So I was very happy. Appa teased me, saying, 'At least leave a little room for aeration, putta.'

Ignoring Appa, I put on my new garment and asked, 'How do I look, Amma?'

She gently touched my cheeks and said, 'So cute that my own drishti will happen, I'm afraid,' and cracked her knuckles on her temples.

'See how your Amma wards off all evil eyes?' quipped Appa.

At the time of peeing in the school, as I slid two shorts down in succession, I felt a certain pride in growing up.

That was the last time. I never became a chaddi rascal after that. But Akka kept teasing me about it now and then. Whenever some little kid was seen walking home crying after becoming a chaddi rascal at school, she'd say, 'Putta, look, your kid brother seems to be having a problem; go pacify him,' or some such thing. But when I started Class Eight, she made fun of me, saying, 'Our putta won't be a chaddi rascal anymore; if at all, he'd be a pant rascal henceforth,' and guffawed. I went wild and fought with her, pulling her plaits and all. While seeing me off to a faraway town where I went to study engineering after my Class Twelve exams, she pulled my leg saying, 'Putta, you better be careful in case you end up pooping in the class. Amma can't come all the way to your college to clean up.'

Akka got married when I was in second year of college. By the time I got a job in Bangalore (now Bengaluru) and was able to 'settle down' in a rented apartment, Akka's son had started going to school. 'Clearly, your nephew has taken after his maternal uncle. I have already visited his school twice to clean up,' Akka said over the phone one day, giggling endlessly.

It had already been fifteen years since Amma had become diabetic. Appa was also more or less confined to home after his retirement. 'I don't know why you need to stay by yourselves anymore. Just come and stay with me,' I insisted and brought them to Bangalore.

Although Akka kept saying that she'd come and stay peacefully in her tavaru mane for at least a month, she couldn't manage a visit to her maternal house for the next three years. A small child at home, her husband's office and her son's school—one or the other preoccupation came in the way of her plans.

Finally, one day I called her and said, 'Akka, Amma has been a bit under the weather of late. If you could come down for a few days and be with her, it might help her to perk up a bit.'

After that, she came down to visit us with her son. My nephew was already in Class Seven. 'Do you still keep becoming a chaddi rascal, raja…?' I bantered.

'Hey, keep quiet, Mama,' my nephew blushed in response.

My parents were having a great time with their grandson and enjoyed having so many people at home after many years; nobody realized how time flew.

'I'll wash all the laundry in the washing machine here only. It will save me the trouble of washing them manually at home,' Akka said on the day she was to return home on the Hampi Express. In about ten minutes, when the washer's tub filled with water and began to spin, a foul odour spread throughout the house. None of us could identify where the stench was coming from.

'It's coming from the washing machine!' said my nephew, cracking the mystery.

'How shameless, raja! You are already in Class Seven, mind you!' Akka screamed at her son.

'Shut up, Amma … it's not me,' my nephew retorted angrily.

'Don't lie! You are the only child in this house,' argued Akka.

'God promise, it's not me!' he insisted.

The 'God promise' seemed to cut some ice with Akka. Her gaze of suspicion slowly turned towards me! 'Putta…'

'Come on, Akka, what nonsense!' I interjected before she could say anything more.

'Could it be the cat?' wondered Akka.

'I know who has done it!' yelled my nephew.

'Tell me who?' asked Akka.

'It's Ajji! When I hugged her in the morning, she was stinking. It's her, I know,' insisted the boy.

'Why are you simply blaming it on me, you liar!' Amma retorted angrily.

'I'm no liar; you are the liar. I know it's you; you are just not admitting to it,' he shot back.

'No ... no, it's not me; your son is lying.' Amma complained to Akka, rather helplessly.

'It's you … it's you ... it's you!' he yelled repeatedly. Akka got irritated and gave him a tight slap. The boy started bawling loudly.

I directly went to the washing machine and opened its lid. I took out Amma's saree and found evidence that supported my nephew's allegations. I was infuriated. Somewhere deep down, an ugly thought that Amma was a country bumpkin must have been lurking in me, for I started speaking to her rudely.

'Have you no shame? Aren't you old enough to understand such a simple thing? Even my work clothes have been put into that machine. Shall I wear those stinking clothes to my office tomorrow? What will the neighbours think if they come to know of such a thing? This is Bangalore, not your Bellary! You need to maintain some standards to live in apartments like these. This is ridiculous!' I yelled with disgust and anger.

Amma looked down in silence.

Akka had to leave soon to catch her train. After placating me, Akka quickly washed the clothes in the bathroom. Wringing them tightly, she made a bundle of the damp clothes. There wasn't enough time to eat food, let alone dry the clothes. She quickly got ready to leave. I went to the railway station to see her off. Hiring a rickshaw for Akka and my nephew, I followed them on my bike.

After making them board the train, I ran over to a nearby canteen on the platform to get some curd rice packed for them. As soon as I passed the food packet to Akka through the window, the train started chugging away slowly.

As I walked along the moving train on the platform, my preachy Akka started advising me. 'Don't get angry and shout at Amma; her health is no longer what it used to be. Who knows if her muscles have the strength to hold back or not? After all, she isn't getting any younger. Even my mother-in-law had issues with her bowel control ...'

As she was speaking, the train picked up pace and zoomed away. Feeling tired, I sat down on a bench nearby. I was feeling remorseful for having shouted at Amma. I felt depressed by the detestable episode that had taken place at home.

When I returned, Appa was waiting for me at the end of the alley. Seeing my bike, he waved his hand at me to stop. I stopped and walked with Appa, pushing my bike along.

'Your mother is very upset. She's squatting silently in the room. She isn't even talking to me. Go and soothe her a bit.

Looks like the bloody diabetes is troubling her a lot these days,' pleaded Appa.

Amma was lying down alone in the room.

'Amma,' I called out to her as I entered.

She sat up.

I warmly took both her hands into mine and said, 'Sorry, Amma, I don't know what had come over me; in a fit of anger I blabbered all nonsense. Please forgive me, Amma.'

She started weeping. 'You scolded me …' Amma cribbed like a baby.

'Sorry, I'll never ever scold you again,' I assured, patting her back.

'It happened in the saree without my knowledge. I didn't put it in the machine knowingly…' She started crying again.

'Don't cry, everything is going to be alright. Let's go and see the doctor tomorrow. Now stop crying, please. Don't worry, I'm here to take care of you. Come, let's have lunch now,' I consoled her.

The next day, I saw her washing her saree and blouse by hand in the bathroom. 'Why are you washing clothes, Amma?' I asked.

'I think it's best if I wash my own clothes, putta … sometimes it's happening unknowingly. It won't be nice if my clothes get mixed up with your office clothes,' she said.

'I'll try to find someone to wash the clothes,' I said.

'No need to simply squander money for just a couple of clothes of mine. Don't you worry, I'm quite used to washing heaps and heaps of clothes,' she said, smiling through her wrinkled face.

And so it was going forward. Occasionally, if she was tired, she'd come with her saree, show it to me and say, 'Look, today I haven't pooped or anything. Is it alright if I put this in the machine?'

My heart would wrench. 'Oh come on, Amma, do you need to ask me for all these things?' I'd reply, my eyes moist and voice choking.

The doctor who examined Amma did not turn out to be of much help. 'Her diabetes has aggravated. It's because of that. The family should take care,' said the doctor.

Amma virtually stopped going out of the house. Once in a while, Appa and Amma would take a train and go to our hometown. I always made it a point to accompany them on those trips. Occasionally, if I couldn't join them for whatever reason, I would advise them, 'Be careful while going to the paikhana during the night. It's risky to move about in a moving train. You better avoid using the toilet when the train is moving.'

Whenever I could not join my parents on these trips, I just couldn't sleep peacefully. Even if I did fall asleep, I would suddenly bolt awake, having some dreadful nightmare. I'd stay restless even the next day till I would get the confirmation that they had reached home safely.

Once, while buying groceries at the supermarket, adult diapers caught my attention, and I bought a packet immediately. However, I felt awkward asking Amma to wear it and hid it in the cupboard. The following day, I called Akka from the office and requested her to call home and speak to Amma about it.

That evening when I returned home, after giving me coffee and snacks, Amma said, 'Give me whatever it is you've brought after you finish eating. I'll wear it.'

I took out the packet from the cupboard and gave it to her. But apparently Amma couldn't wear it herself. When I suggested seeking Appa's help, she refused, saying, 'No, no, don't ask him, I feel shy.'

Finally, I demonstrated the process by wearing the diaper over my trousers. Amma went into her room and returned wearing it.

'No more hassles. See how there's a solution for every problem here!' I said, beaming with pride.

But the next day, Amma had rashes on her body. Her groin area around the diaper had turned red due to allergy. I took her to the doctor immediately. He reprimanded me for being careless. 'Don't you know that she's diabetic? Her wounds won't heal that easily. She has erythema now. Couldn't you have asked me first?' he said, irritated. It took nearly a month for the rashes to heal.

When I bought my first car, Amma emphatically refused to set her foot in it.

'Let's at least go to the temple in the new car once, Amma. Don't worry, nothing bad is going to happen,' I insisted.

After some persuasion, she agreed. But later I regretted forcing her against her wishes. Just as the priest was performing the aarti, Amma said, 'Oh it's coming…' and started scuttling towards the main entrance of the temple. I understood the situation and started running behind her. Watching the two of us run, many people followed.

Although Amma had crossed the entrance, on her way out a couple of faecal pieces were found. The devotees were aghast. People started shouting at me.

'Please forgive us, she is unwell. I'm sorry, I will clean everything. Please forgive me,' I begged with folded hands.

Everyone wrinkled their noses and moved away. I ran over to the car, and fetched a piece of cloth and a newspaper. I then got the water from the temple tap, washed everything and wiped the floor clean.

I couldn't find Amma when I came out of the temple. I looked around but she wasn't seen in the vicinity. I got scared and started looking for her in the nearby lanes. But I couldn't find her. I wasn't sure if Amma knew our phone number or home address. It was a crowded place. Like a madman, I kept looking for her in the same lanes repeatedly. 'Amma … don't go anywhere, Amma, please stay nearby … I'm right here,' I kept muttering to myself.

Although I enquired with the people sitting at the entrance of the temple, no one seemed to have seen her. Expecting her to return to the main entrance of the temple, I waited there for some time. But there was no sign of Amma. I again started searching for her in all the lanes and alleys around the temple. After a while, I saw her sitting on a parapet at a distance. I was extremely happy that I had finally found her.

Almost running towards her, I screamed with both joy and anger, 'Why did you come so far, Amma? I've been searching for you all over!'

'I wandered a bit looking for a paikhana and lost my way, putta. When I thought of coming back to you, I couldn't find the temple,' she said in desperation.

I held her face against my chest and said, 'What would be my fate if I hadn't found you, Amma? You hardly know these big cities.'

I then held her hands and walked her up to my car that was parked near the temple. But Amma refused to sit inside. 'It's a new car, putta, book a rickshaw for me,' she said.

Gently shoving her into the car, I stroked her head and said, 'You're more important to me than everything else in this world, Amma.'

Amma's problem didn't spare her even when Appa passed away. One day, when Appa, Amma and I were joyfully having dinner, Appa started rolling his eyes upwards as a grain of rice entered his windpipe. Although Amma and I kept urging him to have some water, he didn't respond. When Appa tilted his neck, Amma realized that it was all over and yelled, 'Putta, we have lost your father!' and quickly ran to the paikhana.

I heard Amma crying loudly in the toilet. Making Appa lie on the floor, I walked up to the toilet door and pleaded to her, 'Amma, don't cry.' But she started crying even more loudly.

Not knowing what to do, I tried to gently push the door.

'No, no, please don't come in,' she implored.

After Appa's death, Amma went through a rough time. Every morning when I left for the office, she'd come up to the door to latch it up. I found it hard to look into her eyes. She would stay alone at home till I returned in the evening. Once, a colleague in the office casually asked me, 'Have you heard? There's been a murder in your neighbourhood. I just got a call from my brother-in-law who lives close to your house.

It seems before robbing the house, the bastards killed the elderly lady who apparently lived there alone.'

I shuddered upon hearing that and immediately tried calling home. But the phone was engaged. Although I tried repeatedly, the call didn't go through. I had a sinking feeling that didn't let me stay in the office anymore. I quickly got into my car and left for home. I found Amma sleeping peacefully on the couch.

'How come you're home so early?' she asked.

'You are doing fine, right?' I asked. I didn't speak of the tragedy that had taken place somewhere nearby.

When I checked the phone, I found that the receiver was not properly placed on the cradle. Perhaps, Amma hadn't placed it right after answering some sales call.

The next day, the first thing I did was to request my office to send me on an on-site assignment abroad, even if it was for a short one-year project. As though they were waiting for my request, my name was immediately approved for a two-year project in England. I took Amma and dropped her at Akka's house as I had planned.

'Although I don't wish to go, my company is pressuring me, Amma. I hate staying away from you. But I'm quite helpless in this case. Despite my best efforts, I couldn't avoid this assignment. Anyway, don't worry, I'll be back in a couple of months,' I assured her.

Before returning home, when I touched her feet to get her blessings, she stroked my hair and tearfully said, 'I don't know whether I'll get to see you again or not …'

As Amma had feared, I didn't see her after that. In about four months, in the wee hours of the morning, I received the bad news of Amma's demise. Having gone to the paikhana in the morning, she had succumbed to a heart attack right there.

'Since I won't be able to reach home until tomorrow evening, there's no need to wait for me for the funeral,' I texted.

While I waited for my flight at the Heathrow Airport, I felt unbearable agony. I didn't want to draw the attention of the people around me by crying loudly, so I clenched my lips and fists, and covered my mouth with my handkerchief. However, tears kept flowing down non-stop.

All the relatives were already there by the time I arrived. My cousin had performed the funeral rites on my behalf. On the third day, we went to the cremation ground to collect Amma's asthi. Amma had been burnt to ashes, leaving no trace behind. At a distance, I could see that they had donned Amma's saree on a babul tree. It was fluttering wildly in the wind.

The next day, when I was taking a dump in the paikhana, I noticed an abstract figure on the door. It wasn't clear to me in the dark. Later, I examined it in the light. The impression of Amma's palm was clearly visible on the dusty door. One could imagine how the tightly pressed palm on the door had slid down slowly. During the heart attack, Amma must have pressed her palm hard on the door to find some support. I called Akka and showed it to her.

'Indeed, it is Amma's palm, but I hadn't noticed it before!' she said.

I delicately placed my palm on the impression of Amma's and experienced a strange energy. 'Akka, please don't wipe this impression. Let it be there for as long as it remains,' I pleaded.

'No matter how much we pestered you, you stubbornly refused to get married. Had you married like everybody else, things wouldn't be so harsh for you. Now, just thinking about how you're going to survive all alone, I feel unbearable pain,' Akka said, teary-eyed.

2

AMMA'S STEEL KINGDOM

8 May 2006

AMMA HAD NO DESIRE FOR GOLD OR SILVER ornaments. She'd often brush aside the matters of jewellery, saying, 'What's the point in aspiring for something you can never afford?' Back then, sarees were expensive too. Appa would gift Amma a saree either on Ugadi or Deepavali every year. As a poor clerk, he'd have to take a loan to even buy just that one saree.

But then, who can get by without the desire for something or the other? Amma had a penchant for the not-so-expensive steel utensils. As far as she was concerned, stainless steel utensils were her pleasure, passion, fetish, gold, silver and everything in between.

As a city-bred girl from Bellary, when Amma arrived in Appa's house as his bride, she was heartbroken to find not even a single steel utensil in the house. If our town's local legend is to be believed, Amma was quite often spotted silently crying alone on the parapet wall around the well as she rued her fate for ending up in a house of such rustic villagers. In Appa's house, they followed primitive practices like using hand-stitched palash leaves for serving meals. In the absence of spoons, even ghee was served using conically rolled mango leaves. All the cooking utensils were of either brass, bronze or copper—heavy enough to squash one's feet if one dropped them accidentally. After crying her heart out one day, Amma vowed that she wouldn't be a Bellary Belle if she didn't make that house glow with the glitter of stainless steel vessels.

The golden hour of the first steel utensil making its entry into our house arrived earlier than Amma had expected. Within three months of marriage, Amma was already pregnant with Akka. Noticing how she was throwing up everything she was eating, 'What does my pregnant wife wish to have?' asked Appa—love oozing out of each word he uttered. At the most, Appa had expected Amma to ask for a masala dosa from Bhatta's canteen or some garlic chutney—forbidden in our conservative household—if not some smooth red gravel from the Gandi Narasimha Swamy brook. But Amma surprised him by asking, 'Will you get me a steel plate so I can eat my food on it, please?'

In a brutal world where there's no free lunch, who would give a steel plate for free? Will it not cost money? Appa brooded and regretted asking Amma about her wish in the first place. But he had to somehow fulfil it now. How could he risk begetting a mute child by not fulfilling the pregnant woman's wish?

Grudgingly, Appa brought home a steel plate by raising a loan. The new steel plate was indeed a treat to the eyes. Around a spacious crater for rice at the centre, it had four little pits to serve pickles, curry, chutney and sambar separately. They say that the sculptor of the Lepakshi Temple had chiselled such plates in stone for himself and his mother.

The plate brought boundless joy to Amma. Amid all the old utensils in the kitchen, it shone like a new heroine from the tinsel world. Amma flaunted the Lepakshi plate to all her friends in the neighbourhood, proudly bragging, 'My husband has bought it especially for me.' Her smile would be wider than the plate she was showing off.

That plate added an extra fervour to my parents' romance as well. First, Appa would finish his meal neatly and leave a spot of pickle on the plate, and then Amma would also have her meal on the same plate and blush coyly while mixing the buttermilk and leftover pickle. Appa would fondly sit next to her and relish the sight of Amma melting demurely.

After that first steel plate, several steel utensils followed. A small bowl to warm milk, an exclusive bucket for milking the cow, a small water cup for Akka, a large bowl to boil the soup, and so on. I can't quite figure out if the stainless steel prices came down or if people's salaries went up! But steel had caught the society's imagination in a big way. A close relative is said to have gifted two thick steel tumblers for my naming ceremony, with his own name inscribed on both.

Slowly, the old brass, bronze and copper vessels started climbing up to the attic, one after another. Initially, only the essential steel utensils could be seen in the house. But gradually, unimaginably fancy items like the Lilliput plate, used to serve salt during the meal; the Amitabh spoon, used to scoop out pickles even from the bottom of tall jars; the Jayamalini windpipe; the Pakeeza incense sticks stand; and the Kalpana bowl with a floral design also made it to Amma's vast collection.

Earlier, our town didn't have an exclusive steel utensils' shop. If one wanted to pick and choose from a wide range, one had to go to Bellary. Whenever Amma visited Bellary, she'd invariably go to the steel utensils' shop.

On the outskirts of the city, there used to be a factory outlet where things were much cheaper. Amma didn't mind walking all the way to that shop, even in the scorching heat. And, of course, I'd always tag along. She couldn't be at peace if she didn't touch and feel and enquire about the price of every utensil in the shop. But eventually, she would buy just one or two—but even that was enough to make Appa shout at her. 'One day your mother will stuff the entire house with bloody steel vessels and bring me to the streets,' he'd yell in our presence.

At one point, Amma was quite fed up with the blackened tin boxes she had been using for ages to store coffee and sugar. So, when two cute little containers with thick lids caught her eye in a Bellary steel shop, she just couldn't resist the desire to have them in her kitchen. Unfortunately, she didn't have the money to buy them that day. However, the lure of the containers was so strong that she somehow managed to convince the shopkeeper to give them to her on credit. Little did she know that buying those containers would cause such a ruckus at home.

Of course, Appa would always be upset with Amma for buying one or the other steel item every now and then. This time, he was furious because she'd bought the containers on credit. He feared such credit purchases would become a habit and decided to nip it in the bud. He firmly ordered Amma to return those containers immediately. Although she pleaded to him endlessly, Appa didn't budge. For once, his strong conviction prevailed over her formidable perseverance. But she knew for sure that the shopkeeper would never take it back.

Under those unavoidable circumstances, Amma and I had to suddenly turn into door-to-door salespeople for the two cute steel containers. One after the other, Amma kept visiting all her acquaintances in the neighbourhood and pleaded, 'Such wonderful containers, curse my luck! My husband doesn't have the money for them right now. Will you please buy these?'

However, everyone came up with some lame excuse and declined. After knocking on several doors, we finally found someone willing to buy them, albeit for two rupees less than their original price.

On the way back home, Amma asked, 'Will you promise me that when you grow up and get a job, you'll buy me as many steel vessels as I wish?'

I promptly promised her that I would.

Amma always had a precise inventory of her steel utensils. Even if a single item went missing, she'd immediately know and get extremely restless about it. She wouldn't rest until she went to her friends houses and found it. Likewise, even when someone else's box or bowl got mixed up with her own utensils, she'd realize it instantly, and quickly wash and wipe it clean before returning it to its legitimate owners with some snacks inside. Even when no snacks were readily available at home, she'd make it a point to return it with at least a piece of jaggery in it. She always took pride in cleaning her vessels to a sparkle and arranging them in an attractive way.

Once, we went on a trip to Tirupati with all our relatives. Amma had prepared lemon rice and curd rice for the journey. We were enjoying a leisurely lunch in the moving train. After we were all done, my cousin Venu washed all the dishes in a plastic bucket and flipped out the waste water through the train's door. 'Tan … tan!' a clanking sound of some metal hitting the ground was heard clearly. 'Oh my God!' screamed Amma after hearing that sound. A stock check of the washed vessels revealed that Venu had tossed out one of the two tumblers that had been gifted on my naming ceremony!

It wasn't easy to mitigate Amma's angst as she went into a frenzy. She was hell-bent on pulling the chain and stopping the train. Appa had to shout her down to silence. On our way back, Amma took a window seat and desperately kept looking for the lost tumbler. She hoped that she'd somehow spot the lost tumbler, and some miracle would help her retrieve it. It wasn't easy for her to come to terms with that loss.

After that, whenever Venu came to visit us, Amma would give him coffee in the tumbler that remained and say, 'Such a sturdy tumbler, I wish you hadn't thrown its twin away from the train. It's a sin to separate twins, you know?'

With a bitter face, Venu would somehow sip his coffee and leave meekly.

Amma always had a suspicious eye on our maid, Narasakka, who did the dishes and cleaned the house for us. She feared that Narasakka might pinch and smuggle out the little steel utensils kept for cleaning. Whenever any item went missing, Amma had no qualms in directly asking Narasakka if she had taken it home. Irked by her suspicion, Narasakka would reply grudgingly, 'I'm no thief, Ammo … I work hard to earn my bread. I use only earthen pots in my house, mind you. Moreover I don't even know how to cook in steel vessels.'

Eventually, Narasakka found a way to put an end to Amma's suspicions. Tired of her snoopy vigil, Narasakka gifted a large steel tiffin carrier to Akka on her wedding and that zipped Amma's lips forever. Clearly, the expensive gift was beyond Narasakka's means. Touched by the gesture, Amma gave her a good saree, a blouse piece and some money as return gift, and with tears in her eyes, vowed not to doubt her integrity again.

Since Amma's passion for steel was too well-known, most people gifted steel utensils on Akka's wedding. It was also fashionable in those days to give stainless steel vessels as wedding gifts. Amma stacked all the vessels neatly in a large cardboard box. The groom's family chose not to carry the heavy box and preferred it be delivered to their house by some responsible person. A week later, I was chosen to shoulder that responsibility.

The following day, carrying the cardboard box, I started for Akka's house. 'Don't be an absent-minded professor while travelling. Keep the box close to your legs in the bus,' Amma cautioned me for the umpteenth time. Having secured a merit seat in a prestigious engineering college, I was a bit haughty those days. Her cautioning me repeatedly about such trivial things in front of everyone obviously irked me. When everyone was praising me for my achievements, I didn't like Amma treating me like a dumbo. I was all set to prove her wrong and impress Akka's new family by fulfilling the responsibility assigned to me. With a carton full of steel vessels, I boarded the bus. Strictly adhering to Amma's instructions, I kept the box close to my legs. Having settled comfortably in my seat, I opened the gripping suspense thriller authored by the late T.K. Rama Rao that I'd carried with me. As always, Rao's narrative was very captivating, relentlessly rolling out corpses, one after another.

I was stumped when the character I had suspected to be the murderer was killed! Meanwhile, a passenger asked me to move my leg a bit and I obliged. At the next stop, that person must have got down the bus along with my carton. By the time the detective cracked the crime and caught the murderer, the bus reached Akka's town and I finally realized that I was one carton short.

Akka's family introduced me to the entire neighbourhood as the bride's brother who had lost a boxful of steel vessels gifted for the wedding. It's best not to describe Amma's grief and agony. 'You tell me which moron wrote such a rotten book that kept you so oblivious to an entire boxful of gifts being stolen from right under your nose?' asked Amma, abusing a certain Mr Rama Rao, in no uncertain terms. However, I count her abuses among the best compliments Rao must have ever received.

Even before I completed my degree, I landed a good job through campus placement. I was posted in Chennai (formerly Madras), and in about six months, I grew reasonably familiar with the city. Eventually, I persuaded Amma and Appa to come stay with me for a few days, despite them being a bit wary of big cities. Chennai's Ranganathan Street has a huge shop that exclusively sells steel utensils. It's a five-storeyed building with a hall as large as an auditorium on each floor. I planned to take my parents there. But Appa opted out, saying that he would rather stay home. Amma, of course, was on her toes, ready to go. So, off we went.

As someone who regarded the Bellary steel shop as quite huge, Amma was flabbergasted to see the vast expanse of the Chennai store. Except for some space to move about, the entire place was stuffed with a variety of steel vessels. While an array of plates, forceps, pans, ladles, spoons and spatulas adorned the walls, many types of jars, bowls and vessels dangled from the ceiling. Struck by the awe and the stupor of the sight, she held my hand tightly. Putting my arm around her shoulders, I smiled genially. Tears of joy filled Amma's eyes. Every vessel in the shop reflected the two of us standing in that posture.

'Buy whatever you want, Amma,' I said.

Like a kid in a firecracker shop, overwhelmed by the sheer variety, she stood there, confused for a few moments. Then, prancing across the hall, she kept choosing and rejecting many utensils with great excitement. After repeatedly seeking my approval and endorsement, she bought a host of articles. The moment we were home, Amma laid the entire loot before Appa, and gaily described each and every item, adding, 'My son has got all these for me,' emphasizing the word 'son'!

But that made Appa sulk. 'If I had drawn as much salary as your son does, I'd have bought and dumped an entire steel shop before you,' he said, irritably.

Amma didn't buy a single steel vessel after Appa passed away. Lunch served on the Lepakshi plate reminded her of him and made the food taste sour. With the passage of time, all the steel vessels at Akka's house started finding their way to the attic. Porcelain cups and saucers were now used to serve beverages, aluminium cookers for cooking, non-stick pans and bowls for roasting and frying, airtight Tupperware containers to store the grains and groceries, casseroles to keep food hot, wooden forks, coffee percolators, and other fancy stuff slowly replaced steel utensils in Indian kitchens. Once, when Amma offered water to a colleague of my brother-in-law, Akka peevishly said, 'From now on, please serve water in a glass tumbler only. Otherwise, people will think we're lower middle class.'

When Amma died, I was unable to set fire to her pyre but was able to perform all other rites of her funeral in Hampi. At the end of all the rituals, when I offered the Kage Pinda, no crow turned up to eat the rice ball. When all our efforts to lure the crows failed, our maid, Narasakka, suggested, 'Since Amma dearly loved steel utensils, make a vow that you'll take good care of all her steel utensils and call the crow.'

Strangely, Narasakka's idea worked like magic. The moment I stood before the rice ball and prayed as she'd suggested, a crow came flying and ate the pinda. Even in that hour of grief, it seemed funny to us.

Although we'd cajoled Amma saying we would take good care of her steel vessels, we couldn't fulfil that promise. 'Where do I store such a heap of steel vessels, putta? I'm sorry, I don't want them,' Akka renounced. I, too, wasn't particularly inclined to carry all that stuff to my sophisticated house in Bangalore. As a souvenir, I took just the Lepakshi plate. Akka took one tumbler. We washed our hands off them by donating some to a mutt, and gave away the rest to some of our relatives and Narasakka. Even today, when I come across any steel utensil store, I get overwhelmed by Amma's memories. When I run my finger over sparkling steel vessels, I feel as if I'm caressing her.

3

WHEN ANNAVRU CAME TO OUR TOWN

13 April 2006

DR RAJKUMAR, THE REVERED MATINEE IDOL AND the eternal superstar of the Kannada film industry, had once come to our town as well. Everyone was very excited about the 'God of Kannada Cinema' himself, our beloved Annavru, visiting an obscure little town like ours.

Although Annavru was coming to perform at a musical night organized at Hospet, he was to stay at a palatial mansion of a political leader from our town. As soon as word spread, each and every person in our town thronged the politician's mansion. Fifty rupees for the musical night plus the bus fare to Hospet and back were beyond the means of most townspeople. So, Annavru staying in our town was a divine opportunity for all of us to catch a glimpse of the superstar. Who'd let go of a chance to have a darshan of the God himself in flesh and blood?

I was in Class Five at the time. On that day, Appa had gone to Bellary for some work. I pestered Amma to let me go to the mansion and see Annavru. She herself wanted to go as much as I did. Having been brought up in Bellary, Amma's first love has always been Telugu cinema. But at the mere mention of Annavru's name, like a turncoat, she would become a hardcore Kannada fanatic.

Amma and I started towards the mansion. The scorching afternoon heat was taking its toll. Since we didn't have the habit of wearing shoes, the soles of our feet were burning. However, the prospect of catching a glimpse of Annavru made all our hardships seem trivial.

A huge crowd had crammed up in front of the mansion. A lot of people had come from many nearby villages on bullock carts. People of all ages, genders, shapes and sizes had gathered there. Everyone was eagerly waiting for Annavru to come out and make an appearance. I heard that he had already come out a couple of times and genially waved his hands at the fans. But with more people thronging the mansion, we were expecting he would definitely come out again. The crowd was getting bigger and bigger, as the ones who had already had a darshan were staying back for the next appearance as well.

Amma took me to the place where only the women had gathered. The crowd was cheering, praising the different films of Annavru. A couple of ladies crooned a few popular hit numbers from his films. One of the women enthusiastically sang the masculine number *'Gandu endare Gandu'*, without any inhibition. Other women enjoyed the song happily. In order to protect me from the blazing sun, Amma had covered my head with the seragu of her saree.

'He's coming out! He's coming out!' yelled someone. As if possessed by some spirit, people started rushing towards the mansion's gate. The woman who was singing stopped midway and joined the race. Amma and I ran as well. All through, Amma held my hand tightly. The jam-packed crowd had now surrounded the compound. From the screaming and shouting of the mob, it was evident that Annavru was already in the front yard of the mansion. I was frustrated and helpless because I didn't see anything. Amma's desperate pleas for the crowd to make some space for her went heedless.

Finally, Amma managed to lift me up and seat me on her shoulders. Till then, only Appa had carried me like that. Sitting on Amma's shoulders, with my legs dangling on either side of her neck, I had a clear view of the mansion. At a distance, in the yard ahead of the manor, stood Annavru—dressed in his trademark sparkling white shirt and dhoti. His face wasn't visible very clearly, though. The superstar waved his hand in the air.

The decibel of the cheering crowd reached a new high. An old woman play-acted brushing the cheeks of her icon in the air, right from where she stood, and cracked her knuckles against her temple to ward off the evil eye. Tears filled many eyes. There was a toddler next to Annavru, and he lifted the boy high up in the air and held him up for everyone to see. Although initially there was some confusion, people quickly identified the child.

'Lohith! Lohith! Lohith!' screamed the crowd. (Back then, Puneeth's name used to be Lohith.) Little Lohith waved both his hands in the air. The crowd reciprocated by waving back. After a while, Annavru put his son back on the ground gently, thanked the crowd with folded hands and went back inside the mansion. The crowd too slowly melted away.

Amma brought me down and asked, 'Did you have a good look, putta?' I realized that Amma hadn't seen anything, and

I felt bad about it. As if to make up for her loss, I described everything to her in great detail. 'Was he wearing a gold chain around his neck?' she asked. I hadn't observed that detail.

Her back was aching a little because of lifting me. Sitting under a tamarind tree, she relaxed for a while. I gently pressed her shoulders with my little hands and asked, 'Do you feel better now?'

Instead of returning home right away, Amma and I decided to go to the nearby Hanuman temple. With the sun going down, the heat had reduced a little. There was hardly anyone at the temple—when people had the rare opportunity of seeing Annavru himself, who would go to the temple? The priest was sitting alone in the inner sanctum. After Amma and the priest greeted each other, for a while they had some banal chat about the everyday struggles of life and other things. As she was a good singer, the priest asked her to sing a devara nama. As Amma started singing *'Idu enu charita, Yantrodhara* ... ' I held onto the Garuda Gamba with one of my hands and started encircling it. The sun was slowly sinking.

Amma hadn't reached the second stanza yet. By then, two cars arrived slowly and stopped in front of the temple entrance. First, the politician who owned that mansion got out of the car, and then Annavru himself got out. A couple more people also alighted, and they all entered the temple premises. Obviously, on their way to the musical night in Hospet, they had stopped for a darshan. Without batting an eyelid, wanting to give nothing away, I kept looking at my beloved God.

Inside, Amma continued to sing without knowing who had arrived. Running up to her, I sat next to her and jabbed at her waist, saying, 'Look who's coming!' The moment she saw Annavru at an arm's distance, she panicked and stopped singing. He looked at Amma and, smiling, gestured for her to continue. In a shivering voice, Amma resumed her singing.

I noticed the priest's hand tremble when he held out the mangalarati tray towards Annavru. A person standing behind Annavru passed a ten-rupee note to him. By the time all the members of the party put dakshina in the tray, rang the temple bell and circumambulated the God, Amma's song was complete. As she leaned against a pillar in a corner, I stood clinging to her. Suddenly, he came close to us, gently stroked my cheeks and asked, 'Such a cute boy, which class are you studying in, raja?'

'Fifth,' I replied.

'You study hard, okay?' he said.

I just nodded my head. After that, he patted my back and quickly started to walk towards the car. Once everybody got inside, both cars zoomed off.

For a while, the priest, Amma and I sat there, gloating over the special privilege destiny had bestowed upon us. 'He's so God-fearing, that's why God has blessed him so generously,' said the priest. All three of us repeatedly caressed the ten-rupee note that had been touched by Annavru with his own divine hands.

'Keep this ten-rupee note in front of the God you worship at your house and never ever spend it,' Amma advised the priest, who readily agreed.

On our way home, Amma asked, 'Did you notice those four sovereign gold chains around his neck?'

But strangely, it had missed my attention again. 'Yes, of course, it was so beautiful!' I bluffed.

Every time I passed my exams with high marks, wore new clothes or earned some praise from someone, before I went to bed, Amma would take out drishti and ward off any evil eyes. Being accustomed to the practice, before going to bed that night, I asked, 'Are you going to take out drishti tonight, Amma?'

But she refused, saying, 'No need. He's such a godlike person. If his eyes fall on you, it'll do good only; drishti-vishti won't happen.'

About a month later, one hot afternoon, the priest of the Hanuman temple came to our house. Amma served him lunch and later asked him, 'What brings you here?'

The priest sighed and replied, 'Wife isn't doing well at all. She's been bedridden for the last few days.'

He then paused for a minute, closed his eyes, and then continued. 'I couldn't keep that ten-rupee note, Amma. One should be blessed for everything. See, I had to use it to buy these . . .' he said, holding out a few strips of bubble-wrapped tablets in his hand.

His eyes welled up as he said that.

4

A ROLE THAT ISN'T OURS

12 January 2005

AMMA'S DELICIOUS COOKING WAS ALWAYS MY number one reason to go back home at the end of a semester. But this time, I had two other reasons as well to be very excited about visiting home. First, I had secured first rank in the previous semester. Appa, Amma and Akka had already distributed sweets to everyone in the town and had bragged plenty about my accomplishments. But I was eager to exercise my bragging rights myself. Secretly, I had nursed a plan to persuade Appa to get my photo published in the local daily as well.

The second reason was the black-and-white television set Appa had brought home recently. I was extremely proud, and astonished, about the little magical box that showed films right in our living room. Those were the early days of TVs entering Indian households, and a time when we believed that it only showed films. My college hostel was close to Mangalore. During one of my visits there, I'd had the privilege of seeing a TV in a showroom. It had left me awestruck, as though I had seen the atom bomb itself. But beyond that, I knew nothing about TVs. I was envious of some of my friends who were from Bangalore and would boast that they already had a TV in their house. Now, it was my turn to gloat! I had decided that I would watch TV every day of my holidays. In her letter, Akka had written that she had already learnt how to turn the TV on and off. 'Although your sister isn't as smart as you in studies, she has a way with gadgets,' Amma had said approvingly.

I reached home bearing the brunt of the bumpy roads of Bellary as usual—fully covered with the dust of the red earth. The townspeople came together to receive me at the town's entrance. Amma and Paddakka, a relative, stopped me right at the town's gate and melodiously sang '*Jai jai Ramana*', as they took out aarthi for me. Overhearing an elderly relative Kashavva say, 'A son like this is born from the good deeds of seven lives,' Appa's eyes welled up. All the little kids, boys and girls, men and women gathered there kept staring at me with admiration. With the air of a warrior who had conquered the seven worlds, I posed for the Aarthi.

As soon as I entered the living room, the TV caught my attention. It was heartening to see the cute TV adorning the corner of the room. I fondly caressed its smooth screen and asked why it wasn't switched on.

'Actually, we were all waiting for you only,' said Appa. 'The TV has not been working since yesterday. If we switch it on, only worms appear all over the screen.'

'That's why we were waiting for you to come and fix it,' Akka explained. 'Some dumbo suggested that I call an engineer from Bellary. Which fool will go in search of ghee while having butter in one's hand?'

'Having a rank-holder son at home, why would I pay money to anyone for repairing the TV?' Appa bragged.

'Absolutely!' endorsed shopkeeper Sharanappa.

It was barely a few minutes since I'd touched a TV for the first time in my life. Appa was already asking me to repair it. Our entire neighbourhood was waiting to see me pull out a rabbit from a hat. The story of the bluff master Uttara Kumara from the Mahabharata crossed my mind. The magic box in the corner seemed to be mocking me with disdain.

'Food is ready. Shall I serve you the meal first or—'

Even before Amma could finish, Appa interjected with, 'Oh come on, what's the big hurry to eat? I'm sure he would have had a masale dosey before boarding the bus at Bellary. Let him fix the TV first, he can have his meal later.'

The aroma of Amma's delicious food was wafting in from the kitchen.

Yathnalli Venkatesha came close to me. He had a radio repairs shop on the market street. 'I've been waiting for you since morning, Anna. I'd like to watch you repair the TV and learn how to do it. Planning to start TV servicing as well. Everybody says that the future belongs to TVs, you know?' He scratched his head and smiled sheepishly.

Other than using a couple of monitors in the electronics lab, for the life of me, I knew nothing about TVs. But my ego wouldn't let me admit my ignorance. After all the hype about securing first rank, I just couldn't afford to cut a sorry figure before all the people gathered there.

'Open the TV,' I ordered Venkatesha.

With his experience of working with radios, he quickly unscrewed the TV cabinet and removed the cover. I observed the interiors of the TV from a distance. With complex electronic circuitry akin to the shacks in a slum, it all looked rather scary. Not knowing what to do, I made the tester take a stroll over the circuits. Like checking the quality of the coconuts by tapping the finger on its shell, I gently banged the body of the TV with my hand a couple of times.

'Can you find out what's wrong?' Appa asked impatiently.

'Hmm ... I'm finding out slowly ...' I murmured to myself and tightened whatever screws I could see. I tried to gently shake the circuit boards. I couldn't think of doing anything else. 'Assemble it back,' I ordered my apprentice, Venkatesha.

'Did you figure out what's wrong? Appa asked again.

'Yeah, yeah ... it's just a little loose contact,' I said.

Appa proudly twirled his moustache and looked at Kasim Saab. With a nod of approval, Kasim Saab looked at Appa enviously.

'Shall I switch it on, Anna?' my apprentice asked reverently.

'Wait a minute,' I said, closing my eyes and desperately praying to Tirupati Balaji, vowing to climb the hill barefoot and shave my head if he made the TV work. Garnering some courage from my prayers, I ordered, 'Yes, switch it on now.'

Balaji had let me down miserably. A screen full of worms appeared again!

'Where did you goof up, you idiot?' yelled Appa.

Instead of responding to him, I seriously started to meditate on the worms on the screen.

'Being a rank holder, I thought you'd fix it right in the first attempt,' said Appa, rather disappointed.

'Have patience, my brother; haste is waste, you know. He's still a young boy, he would have erred somewhere.' Kasim Saab pacified Appa. The whole crowd was curiously waiting for my next move.

'Open it again,' I ordered Venkatesha, and he opened it with the ease of peeling off a banana.

I knew that the public wouldn't appreciate a repetition of the old act and was expecting me to try something different this time. 'Switch on the power,' I ordered, and my apprentice obeyed.

I ran the tester over the electronic slum again. Suddenly, the tester glowed. I pulled back my hand with a jerk. My heart skipped a beat. Hands and legs shivered. I handed over the tester to Venkatesha and signalled Amma to come inside with me. She came along.

'I don't know how to repair a TV, Amma,' I confessed in a choking voice.

'You've secured a rank, right?' she asked innocently.

'If only I knew that Appa would publicly belittle me by asking me to repair the TV, I would never have bragged about the rank, Amma.'

'Don't worry, repair as much as you can, and we'll take care of the rest.'

'I don't know anything, Amma. It has a high-voltage current. If something goes wrong, you may even lose me, Amma.'

I struck the right chord and got the desired resonance.

She went out and declared, 'My child is tired from the long journey. Let him eat a little and rest a while. You guys come later.'

But the crowd seemed reluctant to leave.

'Why the heck won't your prince fix the TV first? How dare he refuse to do household chores?' Appa roared.

'Look, God has blessed me with just one son. I've raised him like the apple of my eye. Come what may, I'm not ready to stake his life for some silly TV repair …' Amma was melodramatic.

An otherwise tacit Appa, didn't want to lose to Amma before the crowd and went on aggressively. 'Ask your son to spice up his rank certificate with pickles and lick it nicely. God knows what rotten stuff they teach in colleges nowadays. Today's so-called graduates do not know the ABC of anything.'

I firmly stayed put in the kitchen. Venkatesha assembled the TV and placed it back where it was.

'Venkatesh Anna, just switch on the TV once and check,' Akka shouted from the terrace above.

He did so, and Annavru started singing '*Aaha Mysooru Mallige*' out of it. Everybody clapped and cheered. I was also quite surprised, and curious about why it was suddenly working. But I didn't risk coming out, as I feared becoming a laughing stock.

'What spell did you cast, dear! What a miracle!' Everyone lauded Akka, showering praises on her.

'It's a no-brainer!' she said modestly. 'The other day the antenna was facing towards our Kumaraswamy Hills, but today when I went up to put the clothes out to dry, it was facing the Kurumutti knoll. Yesterday, an army of monkeys had created a ruckus in our entire neighbourhood. I just turned the antenna back towards Kumaraswamy Hills, that's all!'

Honestly, I did not know that the work of a box called TV sitting in our living room like a big, fat pumpkin was being controlled by his puppeteer boss called antenna sitting on the terrace.

Everybody kept praising Akka as they watched Kannada songs. I didn't venture out of the kitchen until everyone was gone. Considering the changed circumstances, I silently shelved the idea of getting my photo published in the local daily. Thankfully, Appa also didn't write a piece on the rotten education system for the Letters to the Editor in the local daily.

True, I failed to fix the TV. But in my engineering, I still managed to secure the first rank by topping the university exams in all eight semesters. The convocation ceremony was to be held in Mangalore, and the college asked me to invite my parents to attend it.

I decided to dedicate my achievement to Appa. No one deserved it more than the man who had relentlessly toiled for our family and had never let me know of his hardships, even if it meant running into debt. I requested the university if they could kindly let my father receive the award on my behalf and briefly address the crowd. They happily consented. When I informed Appa, he declined at first, 'You are the one who has worked hard and got the rank. What have I done? Don't drag me into all this.' But I somehow managed to convince him. After he agreed, I wrote a fifteen-minute speech and gave it to him.

Appa and Amma arrived a couple of days ahead of the convocation. I took them to the Dharmasthala temple and the Sri Krishna temple in Udupi.

'Udupi Krishna will give darshan only to the ones who had played with him in Gokula, it seems. How blessed we are!' Amma said proudly.

Both were astonished to see the ocean for the first time in their lives. In the precincts of Dharmasthala, they were stunned to see that the coins, and gold and silver items shoved in by the devotees in the cleaves of the balustrades remained absolutely untouched! Repeatedly tapping her cheeks with the tips of her fingers, Amma kept praising the greatness of God. In between these temple visits, I also managed to train Appa for his fifteen-minute speech.

However, Appa was quite nervous by the time the convocation ceremony started.

'Never have I made any speech in my life. Why are you pushing me into all this now?' he mumbled.

'Don't worry, everything will go fine,' I reassured him, putting my arm over his shoulder.

The moment my name was called, I went on the dais and requested Appa to come there as well. Shrunken by humility and shyness, he came up behind me slowly. The organizers gave him the certificate and garlanded him. There was a huge round of applause and cameras flashed. I also stood close to him and clapped heartily, while looking at Amma sitting in the front row. Covering her mouth with the edge of her saree, she looked back at me, teary-eyed. I smiled at her.

'My father will speak now,' I announced, and placed the mic before him.

With the certificate in his hands and the garland around his neck, he was trembling slightly. Tears were rolling down his cheeks. He took out the slip from his pocket and tried to read the speech. But he couldn't find his voice. Shedding some more tears, he looked at me helplessly. I held his hand and urged him to read out the speech, but he shook his head. Without any other go, I read out the speech which was in his words. As I read it aloud, Appa kept nodding at every word in agreement. After the speech was over, when everyone clapped, Appa also clapped with the certificate in one hand.

By the time we boarded the Mangalore–Bellary bus, the charged emotions had cooled down. Amma started to speak, 'They just asked you to speak a few words, and you stood there weeping like a woman. Had they called me on stage, I'd have elegantly sung a wonderful Devaranama on the happy occasion.'

Appa angrily shot back, 'Do you think so many people had gathered there to listen to bhajans that they'd let you sing Devaranama there? When a thousand eyes stare at you with clapping hands … you don't know what that is like. I was at least able to stand there, even if it was with tears in my eyes. But if it were you, I'm sure you'd have emptied your bladder and bowels.'

About six years after I started working, Appa passed away. A grain of rice going into his windpipe was enough reason for Appa to exit this world. Amma and I had helplessly watched it happen.

His last rites were done at Hampi. Quite a crowd had gathered for the funeral. Even after the funeral, visitors kept coming to pay their homage to Appa. Each time someone came to offer condolences, Amma would break into tears. Ironically, all through the mourning period, the priests made us prepare a new sweet every day. In the blazing heat of Hampi, by the time all the rituals were complete, my hunger overpowered the sorrow.

After fifteen days, when all the rites and rituals were complete, all the relatives left for their homes. As my niece and nephew had to attend school, Akka also left. Now, only Amma and I remained, and we decided to visit our hometown for a few days.

One morning, she said that she'd make poha for breakfast after her bath. After a spree of chaotic ceremonies that seemed to almost ridicule the grief of Appa's death, Amma getting ready to prepare breakfast felt comforting. Sitting on the parapet, I started to skim through the newspaper.

Having had her bath, Amma came out of the bathroom wearing fresh clothes. 'Go and get some avalakki from Sharanappa's shop,' she said. I folded the newspaper and got up to go buy flattened rice from his shop. But just then I noticed Amma's forehead.

'Amma…' I tried to say but stopped as though stung by a scorpion.

'What?' she asked.

'Nothing …' I replied, trying to hide my tears.

But by then she realized it too and collapsed onto the ground. 'I forgot not to keep kumkuma anymore, my son,' she said, crying.

She wiped away the vermilion from her forehead and slapped herself repeatedly. She looked up at Appa's framed photo on the wall and cried, 'What sort of a predicament have you put me in? I can't handle this!'

'There's nothing wrong in applying kumkuma, Amma …' I tried to comfort her.

'You just shut up, putta,' she said, curtly.

Oblivious to everything around him, Appa kept smiling in the photo.

It's hard playing a role that isn't ours!

5

THE MONKEY COVENANT

7 February 2003

MONKEYS HAVE ALWAYS WREAKED HAVOC IN OUR town. But I think saying so in as many words may offend the monkeys. If a spitter could spit far, Hampi—the Kishkindha of the Puranas—is at a spitting distance from our town. According to Hindu epics, the Kishkinda empire was once ruled by the Valis, Sugreevas and the Anjaneyas of the world. Having occupied their empire now, how can we complain that they are wreaking havoc in our town? That would be akin to the British asking Indians to quit India. So instead, over time, we have adapted to coexist with monkeys. And so have the monkeys.

But no matter how socialized, monkeys remain monkeys, don't they? How can they betray their inherent nature? Peeping through the skylights of tiled roofs and taking stock of the food stored in the kitchen, they'd somehow cheekily barge in and vanish with the whole bowl of food. After finishing the food, they'd lick the bowl to a sparkle and discard it in someone else's backyard, causing blame games and scuffles among neighbours. Knowing which fruits were available in whose backyard, they'd precisely plan their attacks based on how ripe and sizeable their loot would be. Badly dehydrated in the blazing summer and desperate for water, they'd charge at the buckets of water with scant respect for our presence. During Deepavali though, scared of the sound of crackers, they would climb up the trees and sit there shivering with fear.

In the hot summers of Bellary, the womenfolk of our town are excited about making happala and sandige, a kind of papads and fryums. Just like peacocks dance joyfully with their open feathers in spring, our women rejoice by drying out their papads and fryums on the rooftops in the summer. Just as they would arrange various types of sandige on the roof in an orderly way, families of monkeys would be ready to jump from treetops and attack. Although us kids—armed with canes, gongs, empty vessels and slingshots—tried hard to defend the stuff, the triumphant monkeys usually had the last laugh.

Once, a woman in the neighbourhood read somewhere that monkeys hate the taste of hing, asafoetida. She proudly shared her million-dollar secret with all the other women. Enthused by the new tip, the women started preparing fryums and papads with a generous dose of hing. The tip turned out to be highly effective. The monkeys indeed had an aversion to asafoetida and spat back all the fryums and papads they'd put into their mouths. The woman who had shared the magical remedy, couldn't stop gloating, 'Didn't I tell you it'll work?'

Amma was upset though. 'Why do we Brahmins so fondly relish the stuff that even monkeys loathe?' she wondered. From the following day onwards, she stopped adding hing to the naivedya she sent to the Hanuman temple. But despite the hing, the monkeys couldn't stay away from the fryums and papads for long. Gradually, they adapted to the new taste and began eating them as before. Amma felt reassured. 'Brahmins' food can never be frowned upon. It was just a matter of time,' said Amma proudly. Noticing that the monkeys quickly adapted to the hing, she started adding it again to the naivedya for the Hanuman temple.

When TVs first came to our town, people got really fed up with the monkey menace. When the neighbourhood folks would be engrossed in an emotional TV drama, monkeys would suddenly jump on the antenna and the screens downstairs would stop working. Immediately, dots would appear in place of pictures, and people would yell in frustration. Somebody had to grudgingly climb up to the roof and keep changing the direction of the antenna until people from below shouted that the picture was back. Just as people would get back into the groove of the story, another monkey would meddle with the antenna and the whole process would begin all over again.

In a bid to outsmart monkeys, some people tried putting thorny twigs over the antenna. Others tried to cover it with gaudily coloured clothes. A few tried to heighten the antenna using long sticks. But nothing could keep the monkeys at bay. Shanubhog Subbanna decided to abandon all the mundane ways and chose to walk the spiritual path by hanging a glossy calendar of Lord Rama posing with his famous bow and arrow on the antenna's pole. 'After all, it's an image of Lord Rama, how can any monkey dare jump on their master?' he reasoned. But the monkeys, as true followers of Advaitha, indiscriminately destroyed their master's picture as any other piece of paper.

Subbanna was disillusioned. Appa comforted him, saying, 'The picture you hung up on the antenna is just an imaginary depiction of Lord Rama as conceived by some artist. Who knows what the real Rama looked like? Maybe the monkeys couldn't recognize him.'

People in my town had such familiarity with monkeys that they would be able identify baby monkeys—this little one was the son of the short-tailed monkey, or that baby was the daughter of the limping monkey, and so on. Although people identified the baby monkeys by their moms, they were smart enough not to hazard a guess about their dads.

Meanwhile, Amma had cultivated a relationship with one monkey quite well. As an orthodox woman, she followed a religious covenant of strict fasting till she wasn't done with her morning bath and pooja. While chopping the vegetables, she'd need someone to taste bits of cucumbers and ridge gourds, and tell her if they were sweet or bitter. Although Akka and I happily did it for Amma when we were younger, we started throwing our weight around and dodged such childish chores once we were older. But the monkey Amma had befriended would joyfully do it for her. If it was sweet, it would relish it happily, and if it was bitter, it would go ahead and spit it out. After Amma was done with her chopping, she'd give him half a cucumber, and he'd happily go away and return the next day. Once, though, an entire lot of cucumbers turned out to be bitter, which made the monkey go wild. It scared Amma, but she somehow managed to placate him by giving him half a coconut.

Advocate Sundara Rao's mother, Kashavva, loved monkeys dearly. Every day she'd give away all the leftover food to the monkeys. She'd also plead with vegetable sellers to give her their stale stock in order to feed the monkeys. She'd always keep a couple of pots of water for them on the roof of her house. When Kashavva unfortunately passed away due to an illness, Sundara Rao decided to perform her last rites on the banks of the Tungabhadra river in Hampi. Everything was going well until, in the end, despite our best efforts, Kage Pinda didn't happen. All the relatives cried hoarsely, 'Kaa ...kaa … kaa … kaa!' They even vowed to do this and that, if any crow turned up. But no crow came to eat the rice ball.

'Quite a few people have done the last rites here today. Perhaps all the crows have eaten enough rice balls already and aren't hungry anymore,' the priest reasoned.

Sundara Rao wearily said, 'Come quickly and have your meal, Amma. Don't delay our lunch.'

In a short while, a monkey came and picked up the rice ball and ran away with it.

Startled by the sudden turn of events, the befuddled priest exclaimed, 'Instead of Kage Pinda, it has become Kothi Pinda today! What do we do now?'

'My mother loved monkeys way more than crows. Let's assume that whatever happened, happened for the best,' said Sundara Rao, visibly satisfied.

About six kilometres away from our town, in a cave atop a knoll, there is a temple dedicated to Narasimha Swamy. People used to say that a cave was an apt abode for Lord Narasimha. Since the cave is in a forest, there's no dearth of monkeys around the temple. These monkeys are more robust than the ones found in our town. They keep moving around the temple, on the hunt for coconuts and bananas the devotees offer them. Us kids enjoyed watching their naughty games back then.

Once, I noticed a baby monkey sitting on the pedestal of the Garuda Gamba. Since there were no big monkeys around, I quietly went close to the baby monkey and dared to pull its tail, which was lying on the ground. But the baby monkey was not alone. In fact, its mother suddenly pounced on me from nowhere, scratched my hand with her sharp claws, and fled with its child and settled on a nearby tree. I was left crying in pain as my hand began to bleed.

Everyone in the temple came running towards me.

Amma was petrified to see my hand bleeding. 'Did you do any mischief or what?' she asked.

'I did nothing. I was simply standing there. It came on its own and attacked me,' I lied, feigning innocence.

Intensely hurt, Amma showed my bleeding hand to the mother monkey that was sitting with its baby. 'May your family be ruined. Despite having a baby yourself, how could you bruise mine like this?' she cursed.

She tied a wet cloth around my wound and pacified me. After a while, when my crying subsided, to clear her suspicion, she sternly asked again, 'Swear on Lord Hanuman and tell me that you really didn't do anything?'

Not daring to risk the wrath of Lord Hanuman, I confessed that I had pulled its baby's tail.

The guilt of unnecessarily cursing the mother monkey started haunting Amma. The very next day, she prepared a chickpea ambode garland and put it around our town's Hanumanappa's neck. As a souvenir of my encounter with that mother monkey, the scar of its scratch on my hand is intact even today. I've never dared to tease a monkey after that. Let alone baby monkeys, even while caressing the cheeks of human babies, I make sure that the baby's mother isn't angry.

There's a big parapet next to the Narasimha Swamy Temple. If women let their hair down and sit below that, monkeys are sure to come and sit on the parapet and start picking lice from their hair. As soon as it catches a louse, the monkey quickly swallows it. If its baby happens to be nearby, the mama monkey will lovingly feed a couple of lice to the baby as well. But if the woman shakes her head while the monkey scouts for lice, it could get very angry and whack the woman on her head. Though women fear those blows, they still tolerate it, as the monkeys are adept at spotting the tiniest of lice with their discerning eyes.

Seethamma Aunty was Amma's elder cousin. She's from Harapanahalli. Seethamma was known to be rather haughty and hot-tempered. Not just women, even men dreaded her sharp tongue. Once, when she visited us, all of us went to the Narasimha Swamy Temple. Looking at the monkeys removing lice from women's hair, Seethamma opened her plaits and sat below the parapet. Pretty soon, a monkey came and started picking lice from her head. Just as the monkey kept looking for the lice, Seethamma unwittingly shook her head and got a nice whack from the irate monkey. However, she was not the kind to be at the receiving end of such deals. She quickly picked up the tamarind broom lying on the parapet and thrashed the monkey. Stunned by the unprecedented backlash, the monkey ran away screeching.

'Look at her, she doesn't even spare the monkeys!' the womenfolk remarked.

But my God-fearing Amma got scared and asked, 'But, Seethakka, how could you hit a monkey like that? Aren't monkeys a direct personification of Lord Hanuman?'

Seethamma recklessly snapped, 'If the monkey is a reincarnation of Hanuman, am I not Seethamma myself? If any Hanuman tries to wag his tail before me, I know how to cut it off.'

Amma was left shocked with her response.

Customarily, once or twice a year, we would go to the Narasimha Swamy Temple with our relatives and friends, and offer oblations to the God. Carrying rice, dal, jaggery, vegetables and other groceries in a bullock cart, we would cook and eat in the fields next to the temple, and return home after washing all the utensils in the nearby brook. It was usually a whole-day affair.

But did the monkey brigade ever let us have a peaceful luncheon party in the open fields.

Nevertheless, we had developed our own strategy to counter this problem. While going to the temple, we always made it a point to carry a few kilograms of raw peanuts along with other groceries. Before lunchtime, we spilled the raw peanuts in the adjoining forest land. Monkeys obviously preferred raw peanuts over our hing-flavoured cooked food. As the monkey brigade got busy with the peanuts, we also peacefully feasted on all our delicacies.

Even though people normally shooed away monkeys with contempt when they were alive and kicking, once dead, their bodies were quite sought after. While the death of an old monkey who had succummed to age may go unnoticed, monkeys who had died from electrocution always got glory. Even beggars would donate at least ten paise for such a monkey's cremation. Other monkeys would be dumbstruck as they sat on rooftops and trees watching a dead monkey's body being wrapped in a new cloth, with a garland placed on it and a few incense sticks lit as it would be carried away on a wooden stretcher.

Recently, when I went to my hometown after a long time, I visited the Narasimha Swamy Temple. Although there were a lot of monkeys there as usual, they seemed rather tired. Devoid of their earlier activities they seemed weak and lethargic. I felt bad about their pathetic state. So, I talked to the temple priest to find out what was wrong with them.

He explained, 'The government has leased out all fruit trees to contractors: custard apple, wood apple, gooseberry, tamarind, jackfruit and guava. The contractors' keep a vigil on the trees at all times and harvest the fruits as soon as they are ripe enough. Also, plenty of trees have been razed to facilitate mining activities. What do the poor monkeys have to eat? You tell me. As if all that wasn't enough, in the name of protecting the wildlife, the government has brought into the forest four leopards from somewhere. Every other day, they take away one or two monkeys. The scared monkeys hardly sleep peacefully at night anymore. Even if they doze off unawares, a leopard snarls somewhere in the forest, and the monkeys get startled and fall off the trees.'

How can the monkeys stay healthy if they only have the coconuts and bananas the devotees feed them to survive on?

6

THE WEIGHT OF WATER

4 January 2003

I WAS IN AN IMPORTANT BRAINSTORMING SESSION with a dozen British colleagues in a posh conference hall in England when my phone started buzzing. I got nervous when I saw that the call was from home. Usually, I was the one who called because it was terribly expensive to call from India. So a call from home felt ominous. Setting aside protocol, I answered the call.

'Guess what? We have water in our taps today!' Akka exclaimed, her voice filled with joy. 'It's being drawn from the Narihalla!'

Carried away by the big breaking news, 'Really, Akka?' I asked, echoing her ecstasy. My voice was louder than I'd intended. Everyone started looking at me.

'I knew I would be disturbing you at work, but I couldn't control myself! That's why I called …' Akka sounded apologetic.

'Oh, it's just fine. This meeting is not more important than the joy of getting our water in our tap,' I replied.

My colleagues, too, noticed my happiness.

'Any good news?' one of them asked, probably hoping for me to say that we had bagged a million-pound contract for the company.

'Yeah, great news indeed! My family in India will now have a tap and we will have water right in our house itself!' I declared proudly.

Everybody looked at me with surprise.

Unable to restrain my joy, as my eyes got moist with tears of joy, I said, 'You guys will just not get it ...'

My hometown is a taluk centre in Bellary district. My formative years were spent there. I left my hometown when I was eighteen. Akka still lives in the same house there. As I still keep visiting home a couple of times a year, the link has not been severed. I feel my connection with my hometown is still alive only because of my indebtedness to its water.

The mere mention of my hometown reminds me of the scorching sun, ten-foot-deep tap pits, faded plastic pots and the sunburnt people who fetched water in those discoloured pots. I started my water-fetching apprenticeship when I was five. I vaguely remember seeing my mother swell with pride when her friend first saw me carrying water home in a small pot and commented, 'Wow! Your kid has already come of age.' Of course, the initial excitement of fetching water for home vanished when it became a routine toil.

The war we waged for water can only be appreciated if you know a little bit about the water supply system of our town. Unfortunately, the houses that had the luxury of functional taps were few and far between. The underprivileged majority that didn't have a tap had to strategically choose a tap pit based on its proximity to their home and the rapport they shared with the owners of that tap.

Every morning, our whole family had to line up in a queue for water. The place we went to get water from was a little far from our house. Since the water supply came at 5 a.m., Amma would go there at 3 a.m. to reserve a spot by keeping our pots in the queue. For identification, she had written her initials on our pots with paints. When the supply came, the owners of the tap would, of course, get to first fill up their buckets first. As soon as the tap was available to the public, all of us in the queue would fight for the water that was in limited supply. The shortage of water forced us to fight with our own neighbours, who were otherwise quite friendly with us. But one couldn't afford compassion in such water scarcity.

Taps elsewhere and taps in the Bellary district were like chalk and cheese. Usually, taps are found a few feet above the ground level. But not in our district—a tap above the ground would have been just a decorative piece with no functional value. As the water pressure was so feeble, it could not have reached a tap installed above the ground. Our people had found a solution to that problem through tap pits. To get water from a tap in our town, it was necessary to dig down to the water main and connect a service pipe before installing the tap.

The formidable combination of the deep tap pits and the acute shortage of water called for a certain acrobatic expertise in men who procured water in our town. According to Indian mythology, Bhagiratha, the legendary king of the Ikshvaku dynasty, is said to have done intense penance to bring the sacred Ganga river from Heaven to Earth. Our task of obtaining our daily quota of water was no less of a toil. To perform that Herculean task, besides seeking the blessings of Bhagiratha, one had to first scuffle and bully the crowd and secure a vantage spot in the ten-foot pit. Standing in knee-deep water in that pit, one had to pour mugfuls of water into the pot. While scooping, one had to be careful to avoid muddy water from getting mixed up with the clear part. Once the pot was full, lifting it in one hand, it had to be transferred to someone standing above the pit. After transferring, one had to also take the next person's pot and place it in the pit before hopping out.

Carrying the water-filled pot up to a point, one had to exchange it for an empty pot with one's ally and rush back to the pit for more water. The ally, in the meantime, had to follow the relay pattern with our other teammates to make sure that the water reached home. Amid anxious exchanges—'Is the boiler full?', 'Do we have enough drinking water?', 'Can we fill two more pots?', 'I doubt … maybe just one.'—the clock would strike 9 a.m.

By the time the water-fetching business ended and Amma gave me a cup of coffee, I would be tired of life itself. After sweating heavily, if I went to bathe, Amma would warn me, 'Finish bathing in just four mugs! Don't keep on pouring precious water wastefully!'

There was a tap right in front of our house as well. Every month, Appa would pay the water bill at the municipality without fail. But the water never came. Over 90 per cent of the houses in our town had the same problem. Only a few houses with yards under which the water main passed got some water if they dug a pit close to the pipe. The rest of us had to beg those lucky ones for water. There were no government taps anywhere. The wells, brooks, ponds and lakes had dried up long ago.

Naturally, the water scarcity was much more severe during summers. There would be barely any water in any of the taps; and if supply came at all, it lasted for a very short time. If we were desperate for two pots of water, the tap owners would allow us just one. Every member of our family would wait in queue at different houses for the water taps; we'd try every trick in our arsenal to evoke their sympathy for a pot of water. Appa and Amma always tried to be extra nice to the families that had the water taps.

However, the quality of the water procured with such great difficulty was pathetic. Digging the pit all the way up to the main pipe, they'd leave open the hole drilled for it. All the slush, dirt and mud would get into it. Then there were those random stinky channels, open drainage, right next to the tap pits. The first batch of water that came through would be so filthy that one couldn't use it even for washing purposes. The force of the water would also be pitifully low. It would require someone to put a plastic pipe into the hole and suck the pipe hard through their mouth. That would improve the force of the water for a bit. Getting a little water any how was the only motive. Nobody cared about cleanliness or hygiene. A pot would hardly get filled, when the water would stop again, and the entire cycle would have to be repeated.

In summers, when the water shortage was at its peak, no one knew when the supply would come. It could be morning, afternoon, evening or even night; there was no telling. Once in every two to three days, the water supply would come unannounced. As soon as it happened, people would frantically yell as if they were possessed, 'Water is coming … water is coming!'

Once, on the eve of my second PUC math exam, suddenly water was released at 2 a.m.. When Akka was bringing in water alone from a faraway tap, how could I idly sit at home? With no other go, I also joined her with a pot in hand. Incidentally, my math teacher was also in the queue with his entire family. Seeing me there, he expressed his displeasure with my sister. 'How can you make your brother stand in the queue when he has his exam tomorrow?'

Instead of responding to him, Akka said to me, 'You just go home and study now. Everyone will blame me if you don't fare well in your exam.'

As the teacher kept staring at me, I returned home. Fortunately, I scored 99/100 in that exam. After that, whenever that math teacher met Akka, he'd banter, saying, 'Had you not brought your brother to fetch water that day, he'd have scored a centum. He lost one mark because of you.'

Due to the paucity of water, people in our town didn't hesitate to stoop to any level for it. They would leave no stone unturned to stop the water from flowing beyond their yard. Inserting empty plastic covers through the small hole, they'd fill it up with sand. When a sand-filled plastic cover blocks the pipe, water gets blocked from flowing further. Greedily, they wanted to hoard all the water in their pit only. And it wouldn't take long for others to also follow suit. As a result, even the taps that used to get water would dry up. When it rained heavily, the increased water pressure would tear those plastic covers, and we would get tattered plastic pieces and sand with the water.

Despite such a severe shortage of water, Appa nursed an irrepressible desire to grow some plants. Ignoring everyone's advice, he planted curry leaf plant, pomegranate, crossandra and so on in our backyard. If we had been spotted watering those plants with tap water, it would have led to major quarrels. So instead, after the water supply ended, we'd scoop the muddy red water from the little puddles in the tap pits into pots and use it to water the plants. The fact that we had to slog even after the whole town was done with the ordeal of fetching water infuriated us. But no matter how much we pleaded to him, Appa just wouldn't listen. If we refused to go with him, he'd simply take off alone to fetch the muddy water but wouldn't give up his horticultural aspirations. Unable to see him struggling alone, we'd eventually join him.

The news of any relatives visiting us would always make us more panicky than happy. If the visitors were also from a water-scarce area like ours, we'd be somewhat relieved. As someone familiar with the hardship, they'd definitely lend a helping hand in our water rigours. True, they would certainly brag plenty about the water scarcity in their village being more severe than ours, but without offending them we would also argue to defend our supremacy in water shortage.

However, when delicate guests came from water-rich, privileged places, we never let them help us. It would be very risky to let our vulnerable visitors try something against their grain and fall sick. A guest getting sick and overstaying would mean fetching more pots of water for more days.

The task of collecting water would impact many decisions in our daily life. For instance, a woman in our neighbourhood had been told by her doctor that she should get her uterus removed. She had been warned that delay in doing so might lead to cancer. But she did not have any children, and her husband went to work early in the morning and returned only at night. Her concern was who would fetch water for her home if she had surgery and was on bed rest for months? So, she kept deferring the surgery till her condition became very critical.

Due to the water problem, people shivered at the thought of holding auspicious functions like weddings and upanayanams in our town. Even if it meant spending some extra money, many would prefer to conduct such events in nearby Hospet. But not everybody could afford it.

In the early days, every morning and evening, Amma would wash our home's main threshold and the front yard before creating a rangoli at the entrance. Gradually, she limited it to only the mornings.

If there wasn't any water at home, it wouldn't be there in school either. Although there was a single toilet for the teachers, it was practically useless as there was no water. All the students and male teachers would urinate in the open fields surrounding the school building. I honestly have no idea how the female teachers and students managed.

When the situation warranted, we boys would sneak through the fence and defecate in the plains outside the school campus and clean ourselves with leaves. If we got an irrepressible urge during class hours, it wasn't uncommon to shit in our chaddis. Although mothers came and cleaned, they'd chide us for making them waste a bucket of water for a job that required just a mug.

An old woman lived in a small house adjacent to our school playground. In a water-scarce town like ours, she was unbelievably generous with water. Even if us boys went to her house in large numbers and asked for drinking water repeatedly, the old granny would patiently give it to each one of us. In that scorching heat, even after gulping bowls and bowls of water, we'd still feel thirsty.

Once, while chatting with her, Amma asked, 'You're already so aged and ailing, yet you give these kids as much water as they want. Everybody knows how hard it is to collect so much water every day. Why do you burden yourself so much at this age?'

The old woman replied, 'Look, I don't know in which life I deprived which thirsty soul of water that God has cursed me to lead my life in this godforsaken town. If I repeat the same mistake again, I'm afraid I might be born again right here. If Lord Rama had been born in Bellary instead of Ayodhya, I doubt he would have really said that one's birthplace is greater than the heavens.'

Employees who were transferred to our town often carried a stigma, as it was widely believed that our forlorn community was a dumping ground for those facing allegations elsewhere. Stories about the transferred employees like 'He was caught while taking bribes, it seems', 'He'd fudged all the accounts, it seems' and 'It's a punishment posting' would be galore.

'Our town is a place of punishment,' a few would brag with pride.

The local guys would joke, saying, 'Nothing deters us from doing what we like. We can do anything fearlessly. After all, as a punishment we'll be posted to our town only.'

After suffering all the hardships for eighteen years, I left my town for higher education. Although I was happy about not having to toil for water anymore, a part of me always felt guilty about having escaped the problem while my family continued to suffer.

Every time I visited home, on the eve of my journey, Amma would call to inform me about the new tap pits that had come up recently: 'They have dug a new pit in front of Narasinganna's house' or 'One more pit has now come up in front of Kasim Bhai's house…' As my bus always reached my town at an unearthly hour, such cautions were very crucial for me to manoeuvre past those deadly pits in pitch darkness. Spread across my town, these deep death traps looked like open graves waiting for corpses.

Though our town welcomed all the modern things like computers, internet, mobile phones, etc., in time, the quintessential water continued to elude us. People's outcry for water remained unheeded. From Cambridge alumni to local high school dropouts, people elected all sorts of representatives to address this issue. But the woes of the masses fell on deaf ears. Despite people bending over backwards for years, somehow water taunted us like a mirage in a desert.

On this subject, nothing had changed in our town in the last thirty years. The Narihalla reservoir has always been close to our town. The Tungabhadra river flows just thirty kilometres away from us. But waiting for water has been like waiting for Godot. Both my parents passed away in anticipation of water coming to our town some day. But the bloody water never showed up!

But today …

We finally had water coming through our tap! I was feeling on top of the world. How could I explain my feelings to these British people? Even if I tried, would they get it? Forget British, even many of my literati friends who were born and brought up in homes with sumps and overhead tanks in cozy extensions of Bangalore, would not be able to relate to such horrific water scarcity. I realized it when they casually dismissed the water woes discussed in Kumvi's *Barigodagalu* (*Empty Pots*) as fanciful exaggeration. I was disturbed to see quality literature losing value at the hands of readers with no earthly experience.

7

SONGS IN THE AIR, STORIES AT HOME

28 June 2005

THERE ARE DAYS WHEN I WAKE UP AND FEEL AS IF AN earworm is buzzing inside my ears. Random songs from films have a way of stealthily getting into my mind. I keep humming that song all day then. I have never ceased to wonder at the magic of some stray song, which I probably last heard in my childhood, mystically getting into me during my sleep. How does a song I haven't heard in so long suddenly find me? Did I happen to dream about the context of the song, by any chance? I wish I could recall. This mystery simply beats me.

Sometimes, I just keep singing the charana (stanza) of a song continuously, but no matter how hard I try, I can't recall its pallavi (starting verse). Since it's hard for me to just set it aside and move on, quite often I restlessly struggle to figure out the elusive pallavi in vain. I don't know why not being able to recall it drives me nuts! Nor can I consult any of my friends, as I'm too shy to demonstrate the song to anyone by singing it. Even if I did, with my poor singing skills, there's every chance my friends would dismiss me, saying they have never heard such a song. So, I'm damned to suffer alone.

Strangely, sometimes even the songs I totally dislike tend to sneak into my mind. In fact, I've been astonished at the way even some lousy songs with dreadful tunes and lyrics haunt me without respite. Songs are hailstorms of nostalgia. With every song, refreshed memories associated with it come flying.

My town in Bellary district is heavily influenced by Telugu cinema. Although we kids weren't very fluent in Telugu, our entire peer group adored the icons of Telugu cinema, hence we were also drawn to Telugu movies. We never had any qualms about aged Nageshwar Rao and N.T. Rama Rao romancing young damsels. Overawed by the grandeur of the kitschy Telugu films, the Bellary audience disdainfully frowned upon the subtle Indian New Wave Cinema that had meaning and substance.

Amma was a big film buff. She and her friend, Gowramma, would watch every other film in the local tent cinema by paying fifty paisa per head for the 'floor'.

'Instead of paying one full rupee to watch just one movie from the chair, isn't it smarter to watch two films sitting on the floor?' she'd ask.

If she thought a certain film was exceptional, she'd give us one rupee, and send both Akka and I to watch it.

For Appa, however, films were a strict no-no. Let alone watching a film, he wasn't even interested in any discussions related to films. But thankfully, that didn't deter him from giving money to Amma or us to watch movies.

Once, the phenomenal movie *Sankarabharanam* came to our tent cinema. Whenever Amma watched a good movie, she would go on praising it for a couple of days on the trot. But *Sankarabhbaranam* held her so spellbound that words failed even her eloquent tongue. 'So good! So good!' she kept repeating again and again. Moreover, this time, she wasn't satisfied by merely admiring the film; she developed a strange wish to take Appa with her and show him the film!

As expected, Appa categorically dismissed the proposal with 'no way.' Amma singing praises of the film endlessly certainly didn't help. But she didn't give up.

'I've vowed to break a pair of coconuts before Rayaru this Thursday if he makes you come to the movie with me. Do not dare to challenge his powers,' said Amma, posing a divine threat to Appa.

He was clearly in a spot, and with no other choice left, he conceded reluctantly.

Amma's excitement knew no bounds. She prepared some fritters, fried some peanuts and packed them along with a little jaggery. She also packed some peeled melon seeds to munch on while watching the film. Draping herself in her grand wedding saree, she dressed us up in the best clothes we had.

Meanwhile, Gowramma got to know of our plans and wished to tag along, saying, 'How I wish to watch the film one more time … let me come along too.'

But Amma bluntly refused. 'For once, I have managed to convince my man to go for a film with the family. Why do you want to tag along with us like a thorn in my flesh?'

Gowramma angrily replied, 'As though I don't know the way to the tent! Come what may, I'll also watch the same show today itself.'

'By all means do, but for God's sake do not sit anywhere close to us,' said Amma, curtly.

Although we were all primped up and ready to leave for the film, there was no sign of Appa yet. Amma grew sceptical, and sent Akka and me to fetch him from his office. But he sent us back saying, 'You all carry on, I have plenty of work to do.'

When we reported it back to Amma, she was furious. Dragging both of us with her, she stormed into Appa's office like a rocket and stood before his boss like a rock.

Taken aback, the boss gawked at us, clueless.

'Look, sir, he'd assured us that he'd come to the film with us. But now he isn't coming,' Amma complained.

The boss summoned Appa and instructed him to go with us.

'Got plenty of work to do …' Appa spluttered.

'You'll always have work to do … whatever it is, you can do it tomorrow. You just leave now,' the boss asserted.

With no other option left, Appa came along with us.

'Oh my God! Will any respectable lady come to her husband's office like this for a trivial matter like going for a film? How disgraceful! If you don't take me to that film, will the sky fall over your head?' He kept yelling all the way up to the cinema hall.

Amma didn't utter a single word. I was surprised to learn that her deft tongue knew when to shut up as well.

We realized that Appa liked the movie because Amma didn't get any scoldings on our way back home. But we didn't realize how floored he was until the next day.

It was a Sunday, and Akka and I were sitting in the hallway doing our school assignments. Appa was going through some of his office files in the room. Amma, who was about to enter the room to get something, suddenly stopped at the door. After a couple of minutes, with a finger on her lips, she tiptoed towards us and gestured to silently follow her to the threshold of the room.

Scrutinizing the office file, Appa was softly humming, '*Sankarabharanamu… Aa … aa … aa … Sankara bharanamu…!*' We'd never heard Appa sing before. We all felt so happy to hear him sing. Looking at one another, we exchanged smiles and continued to listen to his humming. But he quickly sensed our presence and stopped humming. Extremely embarrassed, he gaped at us like a schoolboy caught committing a blunder.

Unable to hold back her happiness, Amma ran up to him and kissed his forehead, saying, 'Oh my God! It has been so many years but I never knew that my husband sings so well!'

She caressed his cheeks and cracked her knuckles against her temple in a protective gesture. Appa looked very coy seeing Amma beam with pride.

Amma marvelled at the power of *Sankarabharanam* that could make even a person like Appa sing! After that incident, whenever there was a talk of singing at any function, she would proudly say, much to Appa's embarrassment, 'My husband also sings very well, though his voice is somewhat thin. But he's too shy to sing publicly.'

Akka is a very good singer. She would always win the first prize in singing competitions at school. We had an elderly Kannada teacher who abhorred film songs and forbade students from singing them in school. But we, of course, loved films and their songs. Akka had even tried to persuade the teacher to allow film songs in singing competitions. However, the orthodox person that he was, he never budged. In one such competition, Akka chose to ignore the diktat and sang '*Joke Naanu Balliya Minchu*' with full enthusiasm.

When she sang that juicy song in high octave, the audiencc got goosebumps. Even though that teacher kept staring at Akka contemptuously, she looked away and finished her song—and a huge round of applause followed. In the end, however, the teacher declared someone else as the winner. Nevertheless, the headmaster who had witnessed the whole programme, announced a special prize for Akka's rendition. Since then, film songs found their legitimate entry into our school's singing competitions.

Unfortunately, Akka grew out of her craze for film songs once she reached college. By the time she was in her second year of college, our parents had started looking for a suitable marriage alliance for her. When we went to see a prospective groom, as usual, Amma started bragging about Akka's singing prowess. So, the boy's family asked Akka to sing a song. She began to sing the popular number '*Cheppalamma Srivaari Muchchatlu*' from the Telugu film, *Srivaari Muchchatlu*.

Though Akka was somewhat familiar with Telugu, she wasn't proficient enough to understand the lyrics of the song. We had all heard that *Srivaari Muchchatlu* was a love triangle in which Jayasudha played the sacrificial lover who let go of Nageshwar Rao for her friend Jayaprada. But little did we know that Jayasudha had sung it while sending the newlywed couple to the nuptial room, and the song meant, 'Tell me the saucy ways of your consort.' Poor Akka had no clue about the song's context, as the film hadn't released in our town yet. She had just rote-learnt it from the radio.

Amma was fuming on our way back. As soon as we reached home, she thrashed Akka on the back and warned her, 'Henceforth, if you ever sing anything other than the devotional song "*Dasara Pada*", I'll break your teeth.'

Although Akka nodded submissively then, she secretly waited to settle scores with Amma at the right time. She didn't have to wait long, as we soon went to see another boy. The buck-toothed boy we went to see this time had a complexion nearly the same shade as the wall behind the hearth. The boy's mother kept gaping at Akka for a while and then asked her to sing a Devaranama. Clearly not impressed with the groom, Akka immediately started singing Purandara Dasa's Devaranama, '*Dharma sravana videtake murkhage / Dharma sravana videtake papige* (Why does an idiot need to listen to righteousness? Why does a sinner need to listen to righteousness?)' Everyone on the boy's side sheepishly looked at one another. And the boy, who had been grinning at Akka all this while, made an arduous attempt to cover his teeth with his upper lip and look serious.

Kamalakka, a tonsured widow, and Kittanna, her only son, lived in a small house adjacent to the neem tree at the corner of Kalamma Lane. Kittanna had lost his wife many years ago and did not have any children. The mother and son lived by supporting each other. Kittanna was a very religious and God-fearing person. He knew many hymns by heart and reading religious texts was his passion. Kamalakka, however, was the opposite. She was an avid reader of contemporary social novels.

Although Kittanna himself brought her books from the library, he'd often scoff at her, 'What's this, Amma? Isn't it shameful that you are reading novels of love and romance at your age, when you should be reading the Gita and the Puranas?'

Kamalakka would fiercely retort, 'Look, you better mind your own business and read whatever you want. But don't you tell me what I should do.'

Once, Kamalakka happened to read Saisute's *Badada Hoovu* and fell in love with it. She'd juicily narrate its story to anyone who cared to listen. Especially while detailing the protagonist Hema's struggles and sufferings, Kamalakka would break down in tears.

We kids would tease her by asking, 'What would you do if Hema suddenly visited your home?'

'Let her just come once, and you'll see how I'll treat her. I'll prepare and serve her everything she wants. I'll cook all the delicacies like shavige bhath, vangi bhath, Mysore pak, curd rice and everything else, and I'll give her a silk saree and blouse,' she'd say, dreamily.

Around the same time, our town tent screened the film based on the novel, *Badada Hoovu*. Kamalakka insisted on watching it, no matter what!

Kittanna was flabbergasted, and said, 'No way! Have you ever heard of a tonsured widow watching films? Impossible!'

But Kamalakka wouldn't give up. 'Hema herself has come to our town. How can I not see her and stay at home?' she argued vehemently.

After a lot of persuasion, Kittanna conceded to secretly send her to the second show of the night. Amma was assigned the job of secretly chaperoning her to the film. Predictably, she loved the film. She was particularly impressed by the song, *'Hoova Nodu Entha Andavagide'*.

The following morning, she started passionately crooning the song. As Kittanna sat down for his morning pooja and began chanting, Kamalakka—who was neatly cooking consecrated food in the kitchen—suddenly started singing the film song. Distracted by her singing, Kittanna missed the rhythm of his hymns and had to start all over again.

'Just keep quiet till I'm done with the pooja, Amma,' he yelled, impatiently.

She was quiet for a while, but quite unwittingly, within minutes, *'Hoova nodu'* began again.

Kittanna missed his rhythm yet again and had to restart. Although by then he was too agitated to focus, he persisted. This cycle repeated a few more times, and finally, when Kamalakka started singing *'Hoovu nodu...Aha...'* for the fifth time, Kittanna lost his patience and quite inadvertently darted the brass bell he was holding in his hand at the source of the distraction. The bell forcefully hit Kamalakka's right hand, causing a fracture. The doctor plastered the fractured hand.

For the next three months, besides draping her red saree on his mother, Kittanna also had to cook for the both of them.

Tippeshi was not particularly bright in his studies. His stepmother used this as an excuse to withdraw him from school and forced him to serve as her lackey, assisting her with household chores. She barely provided him with two meagre meals a day. But Tippeshi was a gifted singer and a big fan of superstar Dr Rajkumar. He knew all the songs from all the movies of Annavru. He was so devoted that he wouldn't even sing the songs of any other actor. If anyone gave him ten paise or got him a meal, he'd happily sing any song of Annavru, exactly like its original. He'd render it so passionately that the imagery of that particular scene in the movie would unfold before the listeners. He was very popular because of his talent.

However, fate was very cruel to him. Unfortunately, one fateful morning, when his stepmother angrily thrashed him with firewood, unable to bear the blow, Tippeshi suddenly succumbed to death. All of us were shocked to hear the news. The entire town thronged to see Tippeshi's body lying peacefully in the front yard of his house.

It was loathsome to see his stepmother dramatically beating her chest and mourning his death. Just about then, Gopanna Master brought a tape recorder from his house and played Annavru's song, *'Baadi Hoda Balliyinda Hoovu'*. No one present there could control tears flowing down their cheeks. Annavru was aptly asking if a flower can bloom from a withered vine. Let alone others, that day, even Annavru seemed to be grieving more than he had ever done on-screen. The only one who wasn't crying there was the stoically sleeping Tippeshi.

8

BIOSCOPE

7 August 1999

USUALLY WHEN THE FILM CART DID THE ROUNDS OF our town, advertising the latest movie released in the theatres, two people accompanied the cart playing the tamate—a traditional Indian instrument akin to the tambourine or the dafli. Rarely, if the cart was accompanied by an entire band, we would all realize that a blockbuster had come to our town.

Although the same band also performed at weddings, housewarmings, funerals and films—from the very tone and tenor of the music, people could easily discern if it was a wedding, a funeral or a film. It's hard to say if it was the musical sense of the audience or the scholarly expertise of the Korachas who played the band.

Something similar happened that day as well. I was sitting on the toilet to ease myself, when I suddenly heard the beats of the band. I quickly washed my bum, pulled my chaddi up and stormed off to the street like I was possessed! As expected, I could see the film cart coming at a distance. Not having the patience to wait for it, I ran towards it to see which film it was.

Oh my God! It was none other than our Nata Sarvabhouma Dr Rajkumar's new film!

I went mad with joy. On either side of the cart, they had pasted various pictures of Annavru in different poses. While in one poster an angry Dr Rajkumar was wielding guns in both his hands, in another he was resting his left palm on his left thigh and singing with his right hand pointing towards the sky. They had put a jasmine garland around the neck of the second poster and had decorated the cart with multicoloured paper ribbons.

Overjoyed, I danced alongside the cart. A few more boys tagged along and also began celebrating the arrival of Annavru's movie, dancing their hearts out. Making the movie a rare exception, the Korachas had put on their colourful uniform, otherwise reserved only for the carnival of Gandi Narasimha Swamy Temple. They looked vibrant as they happily played the band, wearing their dark yellow, red and green uniforms with matching caps. Shepherd Tayanna was frantically dancing ahead of the Korachas' band. Even the decorated white oxen clad in embroidered colourful clothes seemed happy to be pulling the cart for an Annavru movie.

Men, women, boys, girls and children—everyone who heard the sound of the band curiously came out of their homes to see the film cart. On learning about the good news of Annavru's film, they excitedly started chatting among themselves. Even the dogs, cats and pigs on the streets stood dumbstruck by all the cheer and noise. When the cart came near the Eshwara Temple, the priest also came out and stood watching the cart in awe. The whole town was enjoying the happy occasion.

After dancing with the cart for some time, I felt an urge to share the news of Annavru's film with someone who didn't know it yet. I ran home and almost screamed, 'Amma! You know what? A new Dr Rajkumar film has come to the theatre.'

'Has it?' she asked in surprise.

'Really?' asked Akka, rushing out of the room.

Encouraged by their response, I described the film cart, band, posters, garland and everything to them. After I was done telling them all about it, I asked anxiously, 'When are we going to the film, Amma?'

'Let's see, it has been released only today. Rajkumar's films run for a long time anyway. God willing, we will also watch the film,' she said gloomily.

I felt really let down by Amma's lukewarm response.

Dejected, when I went to the backyard, Akka quickly followed me there to say, 'Look, putta, don't pester Appa and Amma to take you to the film. This isn't the right time.'

'What do you mean this isn't the right time?' I asked.

'You don't understand, just don't keep badgering them about the film,' she said.

I felt sad and confused.

The next day, Subhani proudly declared that he'd already seen the new film and instantly became the hero of the class. All the boys thronged around him, as he said, 'Aye, you should have seen the mad rush at the theatre yesterday! People had gathered as if it was the Kumaraswamy Temple fair. But my dad is not one to be bogged down by a big crowd. Carrying me on his head, he cut through the human walls and rushed ahead of everyone. When he squeezed his hand through the ticket counter, he didn't wilt even when his hand got bruised by the scuffle and bought the tickets against all odds.'

After describing the bravado of his father, Subhani went on to demonstrate how Annavru had fought in the film. 'Do you know nothing happens to Rajkumar even if you tie him down with ropes? No matter what Vajramuni does, none of his tricks work with Rajkumar. Oh, what a fight! I just can't explain. You have to see it for yourself.'

That night when Kashavva came home to collect buttermilk for curdling from Amma, she said, 'I can't tell you how good the film is! Believe me, you won't get bored even if you watch it a dozen times.'

Kashavva was a die-hard Annavru fan and invariably watched all his films first day-first show. She believed that the film would get stale if she didn't watch it on the first day itself. 'There's so much agony, I tell you … Two eyes aren't enough to shed tears,' she went on in a choking voice.

'Are there fights too, Kashavva?' I interjected.

'Why not?' she demanded. 'There are ample fights. Wicked blackguards are plenty everywhere. They won't mend their ways unless they get thrashed nicely. But Rajanna knows how to tame such assholes.' She cracked her knuckles, cursing all the villains.

The next day, the vegetable vendor Ambamma came with her own take. 'A must-watch film, Amma. You should see how despite all the hardships, Rajanna lovingly gifts a beautiful saree to his wife. And you won't believe ... Despite all the traps that the raunchy vamp lays, Annavru doesn't stray one bit and remains loyal to his wife,' she explained dreamily, and let out a heavy sigh. 'That's how a husband should be, Amma.'

My curiosity for the film kept on rising. I couldn't help but nag Amma for it. But she kept ignoring my requests on one pretext or another. While walking on the street, if I happened to see a poster of Rajkumar, I would freeze before it. So much so that I would find myself speaking to the poster saying, 'You know, I'm coming to see you soon.'

In school, the number of boys who had seen the film kept on soaring. A few had already seen it more than once. Based on their own abilities, everyone tried mimicking Annavru's acting. Many students had learnt the songs and dialogues of the film by heart. They would discuss the comedy sequences and laugh heartily. Not having watched the film made me feel dumb and also envious of those who had.

I wondered why the headmaster, who used to collect fifty paise from every student and take us to incomprehensible, boring films, wasn't taking us for this wonderful film! My frustration was reaching its threshold. I had never pleaded as much with Amma for a film.

Whenever such blockbuster films released, although Appa didn't watch, he had never cribbed about giving us money to watch them. Moreover, with Amma herself being such a film buff, I really couldn't fathom how she was staying away from an Annavru film for so long! I knew it could have something to do with what Akka was saying about the time not being right the other day. But it just didn't make any sense, and my patience was wearing thin. I was no longer able to endure the shame and embarrassment I was facing at school. I finally vowed to myself that, come what may, I'd somehow make Amma let me watch the film at once.

When I reached home from school, as usual, Amma gave me milk to drink and some snacks to eat. I quickly gulped down both and came to the living room. She was sitting there, sorting lettuce.

I went close to her and said, 'Amma ... Amma, everyone at school has already watched the film, Amma...'

'So what?' she asked.

'Amma ... please, Amma ... I also want to see it, Amma. Please take me for it,' I pleaded.

'Okay, let me think about it, now you go out and play, and let me do my work.'

'But Amma, all my friends have already watched it ... I also want to ... hmmm ...' I persisted.

'What did I just tell you? Let me think about it. The film isn't running away anywhere. Let me see,' Amma said.

'No, I want to see the film today itself,' I asserted.

'Don't test my patience, putta ... Now, be a good boy, go dump the lettuce waste in the dustbin,' said Amma.

'No, I won't. Not only that, I won't listen to a word you say until you let me watch the film,' I said stubbornly.

'Is that so? Who taught you to talk back like that?' asked Amma, placing the wicker pan with lettuce waste on the floor.

She then came close to me and thrashed me repeatedly on my bum. I started crying loudly.

'Now listen to me carefully; no matter what, I'm not going to send you to any film ever. Let me see if the heavens fall down or what,' she said sternly.

I went to the backyard and bawled loudly. I was horrified to see my strategy of throwing tantrums boomerang like that.

Until now she had at least said 'let's see' and had deferred sending me to the film. But now she had declared that no matter what she wouldn't send me at all! I felt like kicking myself for ruining whatever bleak chance I had. Feeling frustrated, I kept crying incessantly.

Akka must have heard me, for she came to the backyard and started pacifying me. 'It's okay, putta, stop crying now. I had told you not to pester Appa and Amma about the film. If things were fine, do you think Amma herself would have resisted watching an Annavru film this long?'

I just lifted my head, wiped my tears with my elbow and looked at her.

Akka stroked my hair and continued, 'Hope you know that Appa's childhood friend Virupakshappa passed away recently.'

Not knowing why she was mentioning something so irrelevant, I just gaped at her.

She went on. 'Apparently, Appa had taken a big sum of money as advance from his office to help Virupakshappa because his wife was terminally ill and required expensive treatment. But unfortunately, some truck struck Virupakshappa on the highway and he left this world even before his wife. Now there's no way Appa can recover the money he had lent. Nevertheless, Appa's office is deducting a part of the advance from his salary every month, it seems. That's why Appa has imposed a blanket ban on all extra expenses like Amma going to the films or buying steel utensils unnecessarily. At a time like this, you should be a good boy and not throw tantrums like a child. At least, from now on, don't bring up the film until Amma comes around and sends you for it on her own.'

Although I didn't quite get most of what Akka said, I understood that my chances of getting permission to watch the film were quite bleak. I decided to not ask Amma to take me to the film after that.

My resolve didn't last too long, though. A week later, just after the school's last bell rang, Subhani came to me and said, 'Today is the last day, you know? From tomorrow, even if you want to watch, the film won't be there.'

I was shocked to hear that! My eyes welled up. As I walked home, tears kept trickling down my cheeks. The moment I reached home, as though some precious thing was slipping out of my hands, I cried, 'Today is the last show, Amma!'

Amma finally felt sorry for me, 'Let Appa come, putta ... Don't you worry, I'll talk to him and send you to the film.'

Highly tensed, I stood at the door, anxiously waiting for Appa that evening.

Unfortunately, as if the sky was angry at earth and wanted to hit it hard, it began raining like cats and dogs. Usually, when it rained, I used to make paper boats, leave them on the flowing water and watch them float; or try to catch the raindrops with my hands and rejoice. But today, I really got irked and cursed the wretched rains heartily. What if Appa was stuck somewhere due to the rain? What if he didn't show up before the show started? All sorts of sinister thoughts began haunting me. I prayed to God to make Appa come home early. I kept bothering Amma by asking why Appa hadn't come yet. Oblivious to my angst, the clock kept ticking.

Finally, I sighted Appa coming from a distance, all drenched. I ran inside shouting, 'Appa has come! Appa has come!'

'Don't you start off the moment he steps inside, I'll take care of everything,' Amma cautioned.

After Appa dried himself, she gave him a steaming cup of coffee. But still there was no mention of the film! I got worked up and started trailing behind Amma, poking her every now and then.

Appa noticed it and asked, 'What does your son want now?'

'He wants to go to the movie, it seems,' said Amma, finally.

'Who goes to a movie when it's raining so heavily? Just sit at home and study your lessons. One can't find two letters if your chest were sliced open, and you want to go to the films?' Appa delivered his verdict.

I was shattered. Not knowing what to do, I started bawling louder than the roaring rains. Appa got all fired up. Maybe some vexed office matter was eating him up already. Putting down the coffee cup violently, he recklessly started thrashing me all over my body. Dumbstruck by the sudden assault, I stared at him helplessly for a moment and then upped my wailing to a new crescendo.

It broke Amma's heart to see Appa beating me like that. She immediately hugged me and argued for me, saying, 'How can you be so ruthless with the poor child? He's badgering us like this only because it's an Annavru film. Otherwise, he's not the kind to pester us to see every other film that comes to town. It seems to be the film's last day today.'

'But where do I have the money for it? Don't you know our current situation? Plus, it's the end of the month. Even if you strip me bare, you won't find a rupee,' Appa snapped.

My wailing continued in the background.

Amma couldn't bear to see me beaten up and crying uncontrollably. Despite knowing that Appa wouldn't approve of borrowing money to watch a movie, she decided to take a chance with the neighbours. Although it was raining, she said, 'I'll be back in a minute,' and ventured out, covering her head with the seragu of her saree. Amma went with whatever little courage I had. Looking at Appa every now and then, I kept crying unabated.

In a couple of minutes, Amma returned despondent. Obviously, her mission had failed. Leaning against the pillar, she slapped her forehead in exasperation and collapsed to the ground. 'I wish I hadn't gone there at all,' she called out to Appa but he did not respond.

After a while, he got up and went to the other room and summoned Akka to join him.

Appa and Akka started scouting the entire room to find some money somewhere. They usually kept some money beneath the folded clothes in the almirah, but it was already the end of the month. They started upturning every garment as they rummaged through each and every cloth. Their efforts didn't go in vain. They finally found a one rupee coin in a corner.

'What's the ticket price, dear?' Appa asked Akka.

'Sixty paise for the bench,' answered Akka.

They couldn't send me alone to the film. Moreover, Appa didn't want to deprive Akka of the film just because she didn't throw tantrums like me. But even after searching extensively, the required twenty paise were not found.

Appa came out of the room and asked Amma, 'We could find one rupee only, check if you have another twenty paise with you.'

Wiping her eyes, Amma got up and went to the kitchen and started looking for money in all the boxes. Appa and Akka followed her to the kitchen to join the treasure hunt. Appa started taking another look at the containers already searched by Akka or Amma. Upturning numerous cans and containers, spilling their contents like toor dal, green gram, lentils, mustard, horse gram, etc., on to the newspapers spread out on the floor, they found a ten paise coin.

'We're still short of ten paise,' mumbled Appa.

'It's okay, Appa, if we directly go to the gatekeeper, even if we give ten paise less, he'll let us in,' said Akka.

Appa came out from the kitchen, pinched my ear and said, 'Now just shut up. If you make any more noise, I'll tear you up into two, mind you. I've given the money to your Akka. Go watch the movie and come back.'

Although the pinching hurt me, I was extremely happy that Appa had given us the money for the movie. But thinking that it would be shameful to stop crying immediately, I pretended to cry till Amma said, 'Now go, wash your face and get ready for the movie.'

Even before Amma completed her words, I ran into the bathroom.

I applied soap to my face and washed it repeatedly. I wore one of my better pair of pants and tucked my shirt in. I asked Amma to groom my hair neatly. After looking at the mirror a couple of times and reassuring myself, I was finally ready to leave.

Every time I went to a movie, I felt that the characters in the movie were also watching us. And this was Rajanna's movie at that! How could I afford to look less than my best? What if in the middle of the film Rajanna suddenly looked in my direction and said, 'This kid doesn't look good.'

I'd never let that happen.

It was still raining hard outside. In our town, when it rains, people fear the slush more than the rains. It makes the terrains formidably slippery. Even as we carefully keep every step firm, the slush keeps squirting from the cleaves between the toes. With the surrounding filth mixing with the slush, walking on the street feels loathsome. Nobody cares a hoot, though. Before performing the pooja, the Rayara Mutt priest, Venkannacharya, tidily washes himself at the well and walks to the mutt right on these silty paths.

Akka and I headed for the movie with an umbrella. Amma came out and cautioned Akka, 'Make sure that you guys keep your steps firm. And putti, take proper care of putta.'

Appa did not say bye to us, probably because his anger hadn't subsided yet.

Just as we had walked some distance, Akka told me, 'You shouldn't create so much havoc for such small things, putta. Won't Appa and Amma feel bad?'

'Arey Akka … look at the rainbow over there!' I tried diverting the subject.

'Where's the rainbow, dear?' she asked, unable to spot it.

'Look there … over the Kurumutti knoll.'

'Oh yeah, it's so beautiful!' she said, cheerfully.

Halfway to the theatre, we crossed by Kasim Saab's house. There's a small ledge on the wall of his house. On that ledge, there was a small idol of Lord Bharamappa. That God was believed to be so powerful that passersby would always touch the idol before proceeding further. It was believed that if anyone went ahead without touching it, the task they had set out for wouldn't be fruitful. So much so that if one is going to urinate and forgets to touch the idol of Bharamappa on the way, even urinating properly would be difficult, it seems! When such was the case, how could we risk going to the film without touching Lord Bharamappa? Akka and I carefully held each other's hands, firmly keeping our steps on the slippery land, went closer to the wall and touched Bharamappa. Then we quickly scooted off for the theatre.

As the theatre was on the outskirts of the town, we still had to walk some distance. 'Akka, you know the song "*Besuge, Besuge*" from the film *Besuge*, right?'

'Of course, I do,' replied Akka.

'Then tell me how many times in that song is the word "besuge" repeated?' I challenged Akka.

'What's the big deal in that? Give me a minute, I'll tell you,' she said, being a sport.

But as she started counting 'one, two, three four,' it all got muddled up. By the time she reached seventy-one and seventy-two we had arrived at the theatre.

It was very crowded already. Although the film's commencement time was over, they had deferred the start, waiting for people who might have been held up in the rain to catch up. But they had started issuing the tickets. Many bullock carts, tractors and cycles had already been parked near the theatre. Even the tehsildar's car was there! Despite the soaking rain, people fought frantically for tickets. Even though it was an evening show, the crowd was massive!

As we were ten paise short, there was no question of going to the counter for tickets. So we directly approached the gate and tried to pay the money to the gatekeeper. But the gatekeeper seemed to be new. He refused to take the money and let us in. Although Akka pleaded with him profusely, he didn't budge.

The song '*Gajamukhane Ganapathiye...*' started playing in the theatre. I got anxious. Next they'd play '*Namo Venkatesha, Namo Tirumalesha...*' and the film would begin! The film was about to start.

'Akka, I think there is supposed to be a fight scene in the very beginning of the film,' I said, restlessly.

Eventually, Akka went to the counter and bought a ticket and asked me to go inside. 'Look, there are ceiling fans on the left, do you see? Go straight and sit below that fan on the second row, I will wait for you here.' She instructed me and kept peeping through the door curtains till I sat down on the wooden bench. After making sure that I sat down, she seemed relieved.

Everyone got in, only Akka remained outside. The gatekeeper seemed to have no mercy. Around that time an old woman came trudging with the support of a walking stick. 'My child, the bioscope seems to have started already. I won't be able to find a seat in the darkness. Will you please take me inside and help me?' she asked Akka.

Akka expressed her inability to help the granny, saying she wouldn't be allowed inside, since she was ten paise short for a ticket. That made the old woman furious, 'Which moron refused to let you in because you had ten paise less? Come with me.'

She held Akka's hand and walked up to the gate. When the gatekeeper tried to stop Akka, the woman said, 'What sort of a man are you? Not letting in a child for a paltry ten paise! Can't you see it's raining outside? Haven't you seen how Rajkumar himself helps all the poor people? No use just growing big, you should have a big heart as well.'

The old woman asserted and walked in, firmly holding Akka's hand.

As Akka led the woman towards her seat in the darkness, she said, 'I've come by bullock cart from Kanavalli. Due to the pouring rain and rough roads full of waterlogged puddles, we got a little delayed. My grandson dropped me here and went to town, as he has some work in the market.'

When they came and sat next to me on the bench, the black-and-white newsreel was playing. The main film hadn't started yet.

'Not bad, my child. Only the government film is running still. I wouldn't understand that crap anyway. So, not bad at all. Though a little delayed, I'm still on time,' the woman said, feeling relieved.

As the newsreel was a bit long, the audience got impatient and started hooting and shouting. Sensing the pulse of the crowd, the manager stopped the newsreel and started the film. The noise subsided at once. As the image of the Devi appeared on screen with a P.B. Sreenivas hymn, the old woman, Akka and I pushed our slippers a little away and reverently prayed with folded hands.

Rajkumar's opening shot created a frenzy in the theatre. People joyfully whistled and yelled their hearts out. Many fans threw fistful of coins towards the screen. The old woman, too, caressed Annavru's cheeks right from where she was, cracked knuckles at her temples and blessed him, saying, 'Live for a hundred years, my prince!'

Just as Subhani had said, there was a big fight scene in the beginning itself. 'Don't you worry, Akka, they will just hit Annavru a few times at first, that's all. Wait till he gets a little bruised on the lips and bleeds, then see how Rajkumar smashes the villains,' I reassured Akka.

Just as I had said, Annavru soon started breaking the bones of the rowdies, and I was on the moon. 'Did I not tell you, Akka...?' I bragged about my prophecy coming true.

The old woman was super excited too, and said, 'Very good, don't spare them. Give him one more, finish the bastards!'

The fight was followed by some family melodrama—something I didn't care much for, but Akka watched those scenes with tears in her eyes, sniffling now and then. The old woman, too, had become very emotional.

'How do you bear so much hardship, my child?' she addressed Annavru. 'How can the poor folks avoid tough times in life? You tell me! Do we have a choice but to endure and suffer?'

Some rascal sitting near us teased her, saying, 'Oh granny, nobody here is suffering or anything. These are just pictures. Why are you crying so much?'

That really enraged her.

'Don't think you are the only one to be blessed with brains, and that God has filled cow dung in the heads of everybody else. You don't need to tell me; I know very well that it's a bioscope. Why the hell did you come to the film in the first place, when you can't even empathize with poor Annavru suffering so much? Did you squander sixty paise only to fool around like this and disturb all the others?' she retorted angrily, and resumed crying again.

Carpenter Nagappa, sitting in the back row, had apparently seen the film a couple of times already. He was enthusiastically telling his friends, 'Look, this is exactly what is going to happen next … I'm ready to take a bet on it if you want.'

Out of frustration, someone said, 'You can tell the story later, Nagappa. Now, please shut up and let us watch the film.'

But that restrained Nagappa only for a while, and soon, though unwittingly, he again started explaining what would happen next on screen.

During the intermission, the old woman bought peanuts for us. Although her good manners made Akka say, 'All this wasn't required, Ajji,' she kept eating the peanuts. Saying no such thing, I also ate the peanuts liberally.

The next part of the film was full of family drama, and I dozed off unawares.

Akka, who'd put me on her lap, said, 'Hey putta, wake up … it's a fighting scene.'

After a while, Ajji said, 'Pass the kid over to me, dear. How long will you keep him on your lap? Your legs will ache.'

I was smoothly transferred to Ajji's lap.

I was wide awake for the climax fight scene. But soon the film ended with 'Shubham' displayed on the screen.

When everyone got up to leave, I felt scared. 'Akka, will you tell Appa that I slept during the film?' I asked.

'Of course I will. After all the tantrums you threw to watch the film, you come here and sleep like a log and expect me not to tell Appa about it? Come on, putta! Does anyone sleep like this in an Annavru film?' said Akka, sternly.

I feared going home. I remembered that Appa had pinched my ear before sending me to the film. He hadn't even come out to see us off. What if he beats me again when he comes to know that I had slept off during the film?

When we stepped out of the theatre, it was pitch dark outside. Power cuts were quite common in our town. Since it had rained today, the electricity department had a very good excuse to take the power off. It was still drizzling lightly.

Ajji cautioned Akka, saying, 'Careful, dear … be watchful. Don't forget to hold your brother's hand, he's still drowsy.' Then she headed towards her village, boarding the bullock cart.

As we came out of the theatre gate, Appa was standing there under an umbrella with a torch in his hand. My heart skipped a beat.

'Why did you bother to come all the way, Appa?' asked Akka.

'All the streets have become slippery due to rain. Also, there's no electricity. I came along to make sure that you both didn't slip and fall on the way,' said Appa, nuzzling my cheek. He then added, 'How was the film, putta? Did you watch it fully or doze off?'

Tears filled my eyes. I pitiably looked at Akka.

'No, Appa, he didn't sleep. He watched the entire film,' Akka responded to him, and looked at me as a saviour.

I felt a rush of love towards Akka. I also began excitedly narrating the film's story to Appa. While I was explaining how Rajkumar ducked the villain's kick and how it landed on one of their own men, Akka was saying that the same eight-dot rangoli that she had recently learnt to make had been created before Rajkumar's house in the film. As we walked through the darkness, passionately discussing the film, when we approached Kasim Saab's house, as always, we touched the idol of Lord Bharamappa before continuing our journey' home.

By the time we reached the Eshwara Temple, power returned and the street lights came back on. I showed the film poster pasted on the temple wall to Appa and said, 'Appa, that's the scene I was telling you about.'

But luckily he was listening to something Akka was saying and didn't pay attention to the poster. I had just realized that nowhere on the poster did it say that today was the last day! Obviously, Subhani had lied to me!

Now, I had a new reason to be scared. Even though Appa had not noticed it now, tomorrow he'd anyway come to know the truth. Would he spare me when he came to know that I had created so much havoc for no reason? Even Amma wouldn't defend me because clearly the mistake was on my part. She might even ask him to give me a couple of extra blows for lying and throwing tantrums, especially when they had no money. I shouldn't have blindly trusted Subhani and checked the posters.

I didn't speak till we reached home. I didn't even dare to tell the story to Amma. After dinner, we switched off the lights and everyone went to bed. But I was too scared to sleep. After I was sure that everybody had slept, I decided to take the only path I knew. The easy path that Amma had taught me.

I got up from the bed and went directly to the pooja room. The idols were clearly visible in the glow of the burning lamps. Joining both hands, I prayed earnestly, 'Oh, God, do whatever it takes to make today's show the last…'

I stopped my prayers right there. Had I completed that sentence, God would have certainly granted my wish. But what about Dr Rajkumar's position?

I felt as if my revered idol Rajanna was sitting before me and crying, 'See, because of you my film didn't run as long as it should have. Had you not prayed to God, the film wouldn't have been removed so soon.'

In my imagination, Subhani and my other friends were also telling me that they had never expected me to stoop so low just because I wanted to save my skin. I realized that it wasn't possible for me to pray for the premature ending of a Rajkumar film.

I came out of the pooja room and woke up Amma. 'Amma, today is not the last day of the film. Subhani lied to me. Tomorrow when Appa comes to know of it, he will give me a thorough beating.'

Amma caressed my cheeks and said, 'Don't worry, you sleep peacefully now. Maybe Rajanna won't leave until I go and see him myself. Anyway, worry not, I'll tell Appa not to beat you.'

She kissed my cheeks, put me on the bed and kept patting my back till I fell asleep. After making sure that I was asleep, she covered me with a blanket and left.

Annavru was all over my dreams that night!

9

SILENT CRACKERS

24 October 2003

DASARA FESTIVITIES ARE OVER FOR THE YEAR, AND one more Diwali is on the anvil. Around this time every year, people begin to grouse about the rising prices of crackers. Brushing aside the costs, the rich continue to burn tons of crackers like they always do. And as usual, the less privileged stay away from expensive crackers.

There's nothing new about crackers getting expensive. Even my father used to say the same thing years ago. My father would ask, 'Which God asks us to burn our money to the ground?'

He would grumble with irritation and defer bringing crackers till the eve of Deepavali. It wasn't difficult for Appa to snub us and avoid buying the crackers altogether, but he feared Amma.

'If it makes the kids happy, by all means let's burn the money to ashes; there isn't much else it can achieve anyway,' Amma would retort mercilessly.

Crackers shops would come up around the town's temples almost a month before the festival. Our Hampi Master too would set up a stall every year to sell crackers and earn more money. He used to bring crackers from Bellary and sell them in our town, usually around the time of my mid-term break. Sometimes, he would ask me and my friends to keep a watch over his shop, if he had to step out. We'd be more than happy to do that. During those times, we would browse through the various types of sparklers, crackers and other fancy items. Our work included showing the crackers to customers, telling them the prices, packing them up and dispensing them. When Appa came to the shop to buy crackers, I would cross over to the other side, and stand with him and the other customers. Even though I'd plead to him, 'Appa, buy this, Appa, get me that ...' he'd say, 'You just keep quiet for a minute and let me do the buying.' Then he would end up purchasing the same old sparklers, pencil crackers, flower pot crackers and ground spinners.

Once, it suddenly started raining, and we all had to run to take shelter in the temple, carrying the crackers with us. Despite our best efforts, quite a few crackers got wet. We couldn't find any clothes to dry them off. Hampi Master quickly removed his shirt and started wiping the wet crackers. He was very upset and began counting his losses, his voice wavering as the number increased. Feeling pity, we removed our shirts quickly and started wiping the crackers too. Amused to see us half-naked, the temple priest standing inside the sanctum sanctorum kept laughing at us.

On Naraka Chaturdashi, we would all wake up at the crack of dawn. Amma would apply scented oil on Akka's and my scalp, and massage it gently. We would then hurry to take a bath. As soon as Amma took out the aarthi, we'd be ready to burst the crackers. 'Wear old clothes to burst the crackers,' Amma would insist.

As soon as Akka and I lit crackers in front of our house, a few poor children from our neighbourhood would run up to us. The moment we lit a cracker and ran away, they'd quickly run towards it and pick it up. They'd fearlessly kick the turning ground spinners and scream joyfully.

Some of my schoolmates would also be among the kids that gathered in front of our house. Hampi Master's son, Kalleshi, would also be one of them. Ironically, Hampi Master's association with crackers was purely commercial—he never bought any for his own children. I used to feel embarrassed to see my classmates enviously watching us burst crackers. At the same time, I would also feel a little proud that my parents had bought us so many crackers.

We loved dancing amid the sparks as crackers burst around us. But I would go wild with anger if anyone tried to step on the wick of a lit cracker before it burst. Once, when all the neighbourhood kids ran towards a string cracker that I had just lit and stepped on it, I angrily picked up a burning sparkler from the ground and threw it towards them. Although it didn't hit anyone, my classmate's younger sister happened to step on it. Her little foot got burnt and she started wailing in pain. My classmate quickly ran towards her and carried her home.

After a while, his mother came to our house and borrowed some Burnol to apply it on the girl's wound. She then came the next day and the next to borrow Burnol. However, on the fourth day, when she came again, Amma told her that the Burnol was over and sent her back. After the holidays, when school resumed, that little girl's brother—my classmate—hit me black and blue, and threatened to beat me up again if I dared tell anyone what he had done. The attack left his dirty footprints on my white shirt. I was so scared that Amma would get suspicious if she saw the marks and get involved. So, I secretly entered home through the back door and washed my shirt before Amma could see it.

Tailor Venkateshi had a crush on the postmaster's daughter, Meenakshi. He'd try every trick in the book to catch her attention. When her brass pot fell into the well, he didn't hesitate for even a moment, and tied a rope around his waist, dived into the well and retrieved the pot. On the day of Lord Veerabhadra's feast, if Meenakshi was watching the procession, he'd pierce sharp needles into his hands, mouth, nose and ears, and dance ecstatically. His favourite trick before her was to put a lit matchstick into his mouth and close it. A minute later, he'd pull it out, and the fire would still be burning! But forget being wooed, Meenakshi never even noticed any of it.

One Deepavali, Meenakshi, dressed in a beautiful silk lehenga-choli, Meenakshi was carrying water home in two brass pots to anoint the family deity. Suddenly, Venkateshi appeared out of nowhere and stood before her, holding a lit flowerpot in his hand. Fiery flowers danced next to both of them. Taken aback, Meenakshi stood there, speechless. The spectacular sight barely lasted a couple of minutes. The flowerpot exploded like an atom bomb, burning Venkateshi's hand badly. Unable to bear the pain, he screamed and dipped his hand into one of the brass pots Meenakshi was carrying.

His wound didn't heal for three whole months. Meanwhile, Meenakshi got married to a groom from Bellary. As Venkateshi couldn't operate the sewing machine for over three months, his family suffered financially. His mother had to come and borrow groceries from our house.

Deepavali meant new clothes for us. Both Akka and I used to look forward to going to the shops and selecting new clothes. However, Appa used to look rather doleful. In those days, customers who bought things on credit were looked down upon. Thankfully, this has changed in modern times, and people use credit cards a lot.

Although Appa paid all the instalments on time, the shopkeeper seemed to treat us with contempt. Whenever we went to the shop, he'd make us wait and wouldn't attend to us until he was done with the customers who were paying in cash. Even the salesboys knew that we were 'instalment customers'. They never showed us the latest designs and new arrivals. We had to choose from old stocks only. If Amma spotted something attractive and wished to examine it, they would refuse to show her saying that it was too expensive.

Once Akka and I selected our clothes, Amma would tell Appa, 'Now, you also buy a new shirt piece, at least.'

Appa would always refuse, saying, 'I don't want anything this time.'

Amma wouldn't relent. 'If you aren't buying anything, I won't either,' she'd say.

'You always put me in a spot,' Appa would crib, and eventually select a shirt piece to get stitched later.

There is another Deepavali from my childhood I remember clearly. Akka asked Amma to get her a chudidhar set stitched. 'It's not a dress for decent people, it almost looks like pants and a shirt,' said Amma, dismissing the idea. Akka was adamant—she cried, she pestered Amma and she even went on a hunger strike. But Amma didn't yield.

One day, Amma came home with a bolt of fabric to stitch a lehenga–choli for Akka. But when it came to adamancy, Akka ranked way ahead of Amma. When Akka set her mind to something, nothing could stop her. She took the fabric to the tailor, promising Amma she was getting a lehenga–choli stitched, and quietly asked him to stitch a chudidhar set. Amma found out only when Akka wore it on Deepavali. Although Amma was furious, she didn't say a word, as she didn't want to thrash Akka on a festival day. But when all her friends said, 'I think your daughter seems to be on the verge of puberty. See how beautiful she looks!' Amma cooled down a bit. She vowed to perform an apotropaic ritual for Akka at night. After dinner, as vowed, Amma made Akka stand before the door of the house. Then, holding a stack of broomsticks, she moved her hand in a circle thrice and warded off the evil eye, saying, 'Doggy jinx, foxy jinx, owly jinx, fowly jinx, piggy jinx, folksy jinx, mommy jinx and every jinx shall vanish, all at once, gone for good without a trace or a dunce.' She then set fire to the broomsticks, and we stood by the door, watching the fire crackle and pop.

Three months later, the Sankranti festival arrived. On the day of Bogi, eighty-year-old Ragamma, a muttaide (a lady whose husband is still alive) had come to our home to receive the Morada-Bagina. While handing over the Bagina, Amma slid the upper wicker pan to show its contents to Ragamma. It contained a saree, blouse piece, mirror, comb and various types of grains.

'Good that you've kept a saree-blouse only; I was afraid that you might keep a chudidhar,' said Ragamma primly, adjusting her spectacles.

'Look, you made us a laughing stock before everyone,' Amma scolded Akka later.

However, for the next Deepavali, Akka got another chudidhar stitched.

Shambhavi was born blind. Every Deepavali, she would come to our house with some crackers. She wasn't very fond of light-emitting sparklers, ground spinners or flowerpots. But she loved the loud booms and crackles that she could hear. She'd get angry if we held her hand and tried to help her light the crackers. We had to stand at a distance and guide her, saying, 'A little to your left, Shambhakka … No … Not so far, closer … Still closer,' and so on until she lit them herself.

'Have I lit it? Have I lit it?' she'd keep asking us.

The moment we'd say, 'Come, come, it's lit,' she'd come running to us and hold our hands. Once she heard the blast of the cracker, she'd guffaw loudly. Her joyous laughter would echo in our ears much longer than the sound of the crackers.

One year, much to our surprise, Appa bought a novel cracker called the 'telephone cracker'. In order to light it, we had to tie one end of the thread to the iron grill of a window and the other end to a branch of our pomegranate tree, which was at quite a distance. If we hung the rider of the cracker onto the thread and set fire to it, it would move back and forth, making a horn-like sound. Although I stood a fair distance away while lighting it, unfortunately a spark somehow got into my eyes and I started screaming in pain. Everybody came running to me. Appa, Amma, Akka and Shambhakka stood around me, urging me to open my eyes. But I just couldn't. Amma started crying.

When Shambhakka tried to pacify her, Amma asked, 'Shambhavi, will my son also become blind like you, or what?' Hugging Shambhakka, she continued to cry.

Shambhakka caressed Amma's back and said, 'Say, God forbid, Amma, and for God's sake, don't utter such sinister words on an auspicious day.'

Appa went out and fetched the doctor. The doctor forcibly opened my eyes, applied some drops and said, 'Let him sleep now; let's see how he wakes up tomorrow.'

The drops felt soothing, and I dozed off. When I woke up from a deep slumber the next morning, I'd forgotten everything that had happened the previous day. When I opened my eyes, I was shocked to see Appa, Amma, Akka and Shambhakka sitting before me!

'Are you able to see all of us, putta?' Amma eagerly asked, her voice shaking with emotion.

Unable to figure out what was happening, I sat there, speechless.

My silence irritated Amma. 'Say something, you dumbo! Can you see us or not?' she yelled, indignant.

Amma's shouting confused me even more, and I sat gawking at everyone silently.

Realizing that this was going nowhere, Shambhakka signalled everyone to stay quiet. She went to the kitchen and returned with something hidden in her left hand. She then sat before me and confirmed the location of my eyes, by caressing my face with her right hand. After that, she opened her left fist. There was an enormous green chilli in it! She cut the chilli into two, held a piece in each of her hands and started bringing them closer to my eyes. Scared, I ran away screaming.

'He can see,' declared Shambhakka happily.

Everybody smiled with relief.

'Arey, Shambhavi, how could you think of such a smart idea?' asked Amma.

'Once, my stepmom had put chillies into my eyes. I had to suffer the burning for three whole days. I had thought then, if only I could see, I could have run away,' said Shambhakka, laughing loudly despite our shocked silence.

10

WRITING MY FIRST STORY

1 May 2003

I WAS IN CLASS NINE. NOW, I WORE PANTS TO SCHOOL—the children in the classes below me still wore shorts, but I was in high school; a promotion that called for the school uniform to upgrade to pants. I was that classic first bencher who listened to the lessons intently and took notes diligently. The moment the teacher stepped into class, I'd collect his books and keep them on the table, earning a few brownie points. If someone hadn't finished their homework, they would be given my example, saying, 'Look at this boy and learn a thing or two from him!' My heart would swell with pride. I'd leave no stone unturned to impress my teachers.

One day, when the Kannada teacher was about to leave the class after completing the day's lessons, I quickly piped up, 'Sir, you haven't given the homework for tomorrow.' I was, of course, asking in the spirit of preventing an imminent crisis from occurring. Perhaps sir couldn't think of any regular homework suddenly.

'We are bringing out the annual school magazine shortly. I want everybody to write a story for it,' he said, and left the class.

I promptly wrote down in my notebook, 'Write a story for the annual school magazine'. But even before I could finish writing it, Sheena, who was sitting behind me, knocked me hard on the head! Just as I was wondering why he'd hit me, a few more friends thrashed me on my back.

'Beat him nicely; the asshole acts as though he won't be able to take a dump if there's no homework,' yelled a backbencher, angrily.

'If we're asked to write questions and answers, we could at least copy it from this bloody nerd only. But now we've got to write stories, it seems!' shouted another.

'How can we write goddamn stories, guys!' cried another, even as he slapped my head with his notebook.

In the PT period that day, no one let me join their games for the day. I was ostracized while walking home after school as well. As I walked alone, tears welled up in my eyes and started rolling down.

Once I reached home, I angrily threw my school bag in a corner and sat down to write the story. 'How many times should I tell you to get rid of that awful white shirt the moment you come home and wear something colourful?' Amma groused.

To avoid any distractions—namely, Amma—I fastened the bolt from inside the room and concentrated on completing the homework. I had no idea what I should write about; even the *how* of writing eluded me.

As I sat staring out of the window, an idea suddenly struck me. My story could be about a student who participates in a competition and wins a prize, but on the day of the prize distribution ceremony, another student would unfairly be given the prize. I set about writing this story, making sure there were no mistakes. Our Kannada sir was known to scold us if he spotted any mistakes in our work. My teacher apparently liked the story very much. The next day, he read out the story in the class and then discussed it in detail for an entire period.

After the class, Rudreshi asked me, 'Will we get questions in the exam on your story too?'

Not willing to let go of such an opportunity, I bluffed proudly, saying, 'Of course, there will be. Hasn't sir taught it in the class? Only, I need not answer those questions.'

My friend Subhani was an avid reader of newspapers and magazines. Once, he wrote a letter to a magazine about a story they had carried. It was published in the 'Letters from the Readers' section. He suggested that I send my story to a weekly. However, I got a bit scared and rejected the idea. But he didn't relent. It took a lot of persuasion on his part, and I finally agreed.

I neatly rewrote the whole story on the single side of a foolscap paper. Subhani scared me, saying that they'd put me in jail if they found any spelling mistakes in my submission. Frightened, I spell-checked the story repeatedly. In my long declaration to the editor, I swore on God's name that it was indeed my own original story. I also wrote that I'd be honoured if they just published it and didn't expect to be paid any money; to kindly forgive me if there were any mistakes, and so on. We gave the school address as my 'from' address, as I feared giving my home address. I lied to Appa that I was going to see a film and got the money to send the story by post. Subhani had also chipped in fifty paise to help me send the story to the magazine.

Once I sent the story, I had several nightmares of the police barging and arresting me because some spelling mistakes had been discovered in my submission. Weeks passed, and nothing happened. After some time, I totally forgot that I had ever sent a story for publication. One morning when I was using the toilet, Akka frantically yelled, 'Hey, putta, come out! Come out quickly!'

She always gets the urge to poop right when I'm dropping the deuce. Let her soil her skirt today, I thought viciously and stayed put.

But when Appa also joined her in calling me, I realized that it must be quite serious and came out.

Waving a magazine with one hand, Akka said, 'Your story has appeared in the weekly!'

I couldn't believe her and stared. 'I know you're kidding—.

'No!' she cut in furiously. 'God promise … See here.' She held out the magazine to me.

Seeing my story in print, I started shivering.

'When did you write a story, putta?' asked Amma.

'I wrote it for my school assignment …' I replied feebly.

Appa looked at me as though I was a warrior who'd won a war. With tears in his eyes, he hugged me and ruffled my hair. Unable to contain his joy, he shared the good news with all his relatives and friends by writing about my accomplishment on fifteen-paise postcards, which he then sent to everyone. From the magazine, he neatly cut out the page holding my story, got it framed and hung it up conspicuously on the living room wall. Whenever we had visitors over, he'd proudly show it to them and ask me to read it aloud. While I read it, he'd keep looking at me with moist eyes. Once, he fondly told me, 'Next time you write a story, give our residence address. Clearly mention that you are the son of so-and-so in it.'

After my story was published, I went on a victory lap of sorts—I visited all our relatives and friends in town. My father's older brother, whom we called Doddappa, also lived in town. There was some animosity between the adults, and we didn't visit their house very often. But now, I was adamant that we go see him. Bragging before people who envy you is always more satisfying than boasting before people who enjoy your success. So, I was quite excited to visit this uncle of mine.

Doddappa was sitting on a rocking chair and sipping on his coffee when I stepped in.

'I heard that you've written a story,' said Doddappa.

'Yes, that's right,' I replied enthusiastically.

'Will they give you a thousand rupees for it?' he laughed.

'I don't know,' I admitted.

'Or will they give you a lakh?' he asked, and guffawed loudly.

I remained silent.

Doddamma rushed out to the living room from the kitchen. 'Look, you brothers fight as much as you want among yourselves. But keep the kids out of it,' Doddamma asserted, and dragged me into the kitchen with her.

But Doddappa wasn't done yet. 'Mark my words! Those tightwad magazine guys won't pay you a penny. I know everything,' he kept yelling.

Doddamma served me hot dosas to eat and gave me coffee to drink. When I was about to leave, she held my hand and whispered to me that I shouldn't go around telling people about Doddappa's rants.

Soon, Sankranti was upon us. For the Bogi feast, elderly *Muttaide* Ragamma had come to our house to receive the Morada-Bagina. Amma covered the new turmeric-decorated wicker pan containing a blouse piece, mirror, comb and various types of grains with the seragu of her saree, gave it to Ragamma and prostrated before her. She then told me that I also should prostrate before Ragamma. As I did, Amma mentioned my story being published in the magazine.

'Oh, that's really nice. Come on, raja, read it out to me,' said Ragamma, and sat down to listen to the story.

As I approached the climax, Ragamma started crying. I stopped reading, wondering what was happening.

'You continue; don't stop,' she said.

She removed her thick spectacles, wiped them with the seragu of her saree and put them back on.

After I completed the story, she told Amma, 'Give me a fistful of salt and a chilli. My own eyes are quite unpropitious … no evil should befall this child, you know.'

She then asked me to turn away from her and began to ward off the evil eye by uttering some indecipherable chants as she moved the fistful of salt and chilli in a circular motion.

As Ragamma was leaving, Amma asked me to walk her home and carry the Bagina. On the way Ragamma told me, 'Look, raja, henceforth never write a story with a tragic ending. You write as much tragedy as you want in the middle. But in the end, everyone should be happy, okay?'

Rukminamma, who lived down the lane, and Amma were locked in stiff competition about almost everything. If Amma bought something new, Rukminamma would not rest until she also bought the same. If Rukminamma watched a film ahead of Amma, sleep would elude Amma until she also watched it. When such was the case, would Amma let go of a chance to brag about my story appearing in the weekly and make Rukminamma jealous? Moreover, Rukminamma had a son of my age who wasn't particularly sharp when it came to studies.

One afternoon, Amma went with the magazine to Rukminamma's house and showed her my story. 'Story writing is not everybody's cup of tea, you know. It's just that my kid is blessed by Goddess Saraswati,' Amma said, feigning modesty.

Rukminamma, being the tough nut that she was, quickly rebutted, 'Oh really? So nice! When your son grows up, he'll definitely become an epigone of Bellary Beechi.'

Amma who'd read *Nanna Bhayagraphy*, wherein Beechi has frankly recounted his struggle with alcoholism was dumbstruck by this unexpected below-the-belt assault. Without uttering another word, Amma returned home and gloomily sat down, leaning against a pillar.

'What happened? You look worried,' asked Appa.

Unable to control herself, Amma started crying. After her tears dried up, she came to me with a look of steely resolve in her eyes and took me to the pooja room. 'Promise me everything as I say,' she ordered me.

I didn't know what was happening.

'Promise me that you won't drink toddy and liquor when you grow up,' she said.

I placed my palm over hers.

'Promise me that you won't eat fish and mutton when you grow up.'

I placed my palm over hers.

'Promise me that you won't go to the brothels when you grow up,' she said.

Embarrassed, I kept blinking at her.

'Promise me, you scoundrel!' she yelled.

Petrified, I quickly placed my palm over hers.

A neighbourhood college student named Venkateshi used to derive some strange pleasure by bullying me. If I was walking down the street, he'd come cycling behind me and whack me on my head for no apparent reason. If I was playing cricket on the field, he'd appear out of nowhere and snatch the ball, and refuse to give it back to me. If I was bringing home milk from Golla's Lane, he'd snatch the milk can, gulp some of it down and return the can to me to me, with a smirk on his face. If I spotted him from a distance, I'd quickly duck into the next lane to avoid him.

One day, when I was going to school, he came to me with a bundle of papers in his hand and in a serious tone said, 'I need to talk to you.'

I wondered what he was up to now. 'What?' I asked.

'Did you write the story yourself or copy it from somewhere?' he asked.

Now I got understood what he was getting at. 'Of course I wrote it myself. Why would I copy it from anyone?' I asked.

'I have also written a few stories. I don't know why they aren't getting published. Will you please take a look at them?' he asked, and handed me the bundle of papers he was carrying.

Now, it was my turn to throw some weight around. 'Come home in the evening. I'll see what I can do,' I said pompously.

When he came home later that day, I made him sit with me in the room and said, 'You've made quite a few mistakes in the script. It's so hard for me to correct all of them. Anyway, I'll shoot off a recommendation letter to the editor and ask him to publish your story. Don't worry, they won't say no to me.'

Later, I wrote a recommendation letter citing my credentials as the author whose story had appeared in their esteemed magazine and sent it along with Venkateshi's story. Nothing happened for several months.

Whenever Venkateshi ran into me, he'd ask, 'When will my story come out?'

I'd say, 'Good stories get published immediately, mediocre ones take a while.'

Some more time passed. Venkateshi lost hope and resumed bullying me like before.

About four weeks after my story got published, I received a cheque for fifty rupees at my school address. The headmaster gloated with pride. During the prayer assembly, he made a speech praising me, saying that I'd bring laurels to the school at the national level. He handed over the cheque to me on the dais.

For the first time, I was holding a bank cheque in my hands. I didn't even have a bank account. I had to open one in my name to encash that cheque. In order to open that account, I had to sign an account opening form. I still hadn't cultivated a signature of my own.

'Even if there's a slight variation in the signature, they won't pay you the money,' Subhani scared me as usual.

I sat for hours and practised putting my signature hundreds of times to achieve the consistency required. The next day, I waited nervously until the manager approved my signature at the bank.

It has been over twenty years since the publication of my first story. Those memories are still etched vividly in my mind. I don't think any of my literary accomplishments can ever bring the joy, anxiety and pride of those days.

11

LISTEN, MY BESTIE, I HAD A DREAM

22 June 2003

SURVIVING AS A WOMAN IS CHALLENGING ANYWHERE in the world, but in the plains of Bellary district, it must have often felt like walking the razor's edge. Persistent poverty, entrenched patriarchy, daunting water scarcity, scorching sun and the burden of societal expectations weigh heavily on our people. Yet, despite these hardships, life must go on. Setting aside our heart breaks, we must find ways not just to survive but to thrive in this harsh landscape. We learnt to see hope in every obstacle and move forward with a smile.

Drawing strength from our ancient folklore, passed down through generations, our women have developed timeless strategies to overcome life's relentless challenges. Above all, they cling to the power of dreaming—finding solace and courage by interpreting their dreams in hopeful and comforting ways.

Carefully preserving the night's dreams despite the day's exhausting demands, at dusk the women seize the first chance to meet their friends. Once gathered, they spread out the tapestry of their dreams and settle down for an engaging conversation. They recount the people who appeared, the incidents that unfolded, the objects encountered, the words spoken and left unspoken, and the animals and birds they saw. Each detail is examined for meaning. These interpretations, however, often diverge significantly from reality. For instance, dreaming of your head being drenched while bathing signals hardship ahead, sitting before an empty plantain leaf after a meal foretells good health, whereas eating in a dream warns of impending illness. Spotting filthy sewage hints at unexpected wealth, while seeing money predicts misfortune. Dreaming of a corpse surprisingly suggests a joyous family occasion around the corner.

Such unconventional interpretations abound and defy logic. None of these women have ever read classic texts like *Swapna Samhite or Swapna Chintamani*, which analyze dreams methodically. Instead, they blend their own insights with time-honoured beliefs that have been passed down through generations, striving to interpret their dreams positively always.

Amma was a great believer in dreams. Early in the morning, while drinking coffee or cutting vegetables, she'd describe her dreams in great detail to Appa or us. It could be anything like, 'The calf cried "Ambaa", so we know some guests will arrive soon', or 'I was drawing a colourful rangoli; it looks like Goddess Lakshmi will come home in the form of some extra income soon', or 'The neighbour's girl was plucking jasmine flowers from the plant. So there'll be a wedding soon' or even

'I saw a cart being pulled in the chaos of some fair. God knows who'll kick the bucket soon ...'

Once, she said, 'Last night, a Brahmin appeared in my dream and chanted this hymn,' and she started chanted some Sanskrit hymns.

Akka and I were in splits. In the first place, Amma didn't know any Sanskrit. Moreover, it was a hymn she'd heard in her dream! We weren't sure it even existed in this world. But by evening, Amma swept aside all our sarcastic banters and set out to meet the priest, Anantha Bhatta, with betel leaves, nuts and one rupee oblation money. The priest heard the hymn, searched through his many books and finally tracked its source.

'This hymn is from the tenth chapter of the Durga Purana, Amma. A chapter in which Goddess Durga destroys all evil. All your problems will melt away like wax, don't you worry,' he said, showing the hymn to Amma.

Gourakka's daughter, Shambhavi, was born blind. Although she'd crossed the conventional marriageable age, she wasn't married yet. Now and then, she'd come to our house, narrate her dreams to Amma and ask about their meaning. There was only one question she wanted answered in her dreams—would she get married or not.

Amma would tell her, 'Don't worry, Shambhavi, you'll definitely get married. The only thing is that it won't happen in a jiffy. It'll take a little bit of time. But rest assured, it's just a matter of time.'

Hearing this, Shambhavi would feel happy and reassured.

'How can you dream of anything when you can see nothing in the first place?' I'd ask her.

Running her fingers over my face, giggling, she'd counter saying, 'When I can make out who you are just by listening to your footsteps, how can I not know anything that is happening in my dreams?'

Finally, one day, Shambhavi got married. Before leaving for her husband's house, she came to our house and said, 'Look, Amma, eventually my dream did come true!'

Her eyes were filled with tears of joy.

It wasn't long before Amma's obsession with dreams rubbed off on us as well. When we woke up in the morning, if we could still recall the dream, we'd describe it to Amma in great detail for her interpretations.

Once, when Akka narrated her dream, Amma said, 'My child has had a good dream, she'll get new clothes soon.'

Akka wasted no time, and began pestering Appa for new clothes. Although Appa tried hard to reason with her, she didn't relent.

He got very angry. 'Do you think money grows in our backyard that I can squander it on your stupid interpretations of dreams?' he yelled at Amma.

However, he had to give in and buy Akka new clothes.

Why was only Akka getting a new dress? Did I not deserve one as well? I made a strong argument about my right to new clothes to my parents.

'But why?' Amma tried to snub me. 'It's not like you dreamt of new clothes.'

'So what if I didn't have that dream last night? I'll have the same dream tonight!' I argued, and forced Appa to buy me new clothes for me as well.

But we were not allowed to wear those new clothes until the next festival. Back in those days, people bought new clothes only for important festivals.

Dreams dreamt by devotees when they are performing service to God under a holy oath are regarded as highly significant. It's believed that if God is happy with the service rendered, he'd show the path to the devotees through their dreams.

Once, an elder cousin of Appa's had come to our house to stay with us. She planned to offer Hejje Namaskara—an arduous form of worship—at the Rayara Mutt in our town. She had suffered a lot in life—she'd lost her husband at a very young age, her ageing daughters had remained unmarried and her only son had dropped out of school. Although she had rendered smaller forms of worship, they hadn't really yielded useful results. This time, she'd vowed to perform a really challenging service in order to resolve her problems.

Rayara Mutt is about half a kilometre away from our house. Hejje Namaskara to the Mutt meant that she would have to prostrate at every step taken—right from our house to the Rayara Mutt. This service had to be offered every morning until she saw that elusive dream.

Atte was too shy to perform her service in broad daylight in the busy streets. So she'd take her bath at a well near our house and start the worship well before sunrise. As there were no street lights, Amma accompanied her with a lantern in her hand. By the time they completed the service and returned home, it was time for us to go to the tap pits to fetch water. But somehow my atte didn't have any dreams despite her persistent efforts! A week passed, and there was still no sign of any dreams.

'I don't know why Rayaru isn't blessing me!' she wondered and her service with more dedication.

After a week or so, my Atte developed severe pain in her legs. It became unbearable for us to see her suffer like that. Eventually, she did have a dream one night. The dream had positive indications. Immediately, the atmosphere at home lightened. Amma prepared sweets and other delicacies to mark the occasion.

When my Atte finally left, Amma said, 'Sister, let's face the good and the bad times as per our destiny. God knows best what to give us and what not. But for God's sake, swear to me that you'll never ever vow to undertake a torturous service like this ever again,' and got Atte's promise on that.

After our annual exams, during our summer holidays, Appa–Amma used to take us to visit different pilgrimage sites. We'd stay at one site for weeks and serve God. The dreams the devotees saw while serving at such holy places held great importance. Even children like Akka and me offered many services. But invariably our only motive to serve God was to pass our exams with flying colours. One time, however, when we were staying in an ashram, I had a strange dream.

Strangely, Dr Rajkumar appeared in my dream. He was requesting me, saying, 'My son is very weak in mathematics.

I'm afraid he may not even pass his maths exam this year. Please lend him your notes. He'll copy its contents and return it to you.'

How could I refuse when Annavru himself was asking? Yet, I decided to be on guard and gave him my notes, saying, 'But your son shouldn't tear off the empty pages in the notebook.'

Just as I handed over my notes, I woke up!

Amma had a ready interpretation for this dream as well. 'Rajkumar, of course, is a noble man. He doesn't have any vices, like smoking, drinking or debauchery. He respects his parents and other elders. Such a man appearing in your dream is obviously a good omen. The outcomes will be good only. But you shouldn't have given him your notes. It amounts to giving away your blessings from Saraswati to somebody else,' she said, rather disturbed.

As I had also learnt a thing or two about dream interpretation by then, I said, 'I don't think we need to worry a lot about giving away the notes, Amma. After all, Annavru has promised to return the notes in a couple of days, which he will. So we need not worry. I'm sure Saraswati will understand.'

Amma seemed convinced with my explanation.

It was believed widely that dreams seen early in the morning would come true. People also believed that one shouldn't go back to sleep after waking from a positive dream.

Once, Akka had fallen sick. Her fever had not subsided even after several days. One of those days, in the wee hours of the morning, Amma dreamt about Akka's recovery. Once awake, Amma didn't go back to sleep. In order to avoid falling asleep, she kept twisting the cotton wicks. Although Appa, who'd got up to use the bathroom, saw Amma awake and asked, 'There's still a long time until dawn, why don't you come and sleep?' she stayed awake.

'I dreamt of the kid recovering from fever … How can I sleep again and lose the benefits of the dream? She's been sick for almost a week now,' Amma told him.

A few houses down from ours lived Savitri, and her wedding had been fixed to a groom from Bellary. About a couple of months before the wedding, making some lame excuses, the groom's family decided to back out from the commitment. Conveniently, they said, 'Our family deity appeared in a dream and warned us not to proceed with the marriage proposal.'

Savitri's parents went to the groom's house, shed tears and pleaded with them to reconsider their decision. However, the boy's family would not be swayed.

Using the dream as an excuse, they turned down the request, saying, 'Actually, we want to have your daughter as our daughter-in-law very much, but what to do? As our family deity is against this alliance, we are quite helpless.'

Once, while sharing her grief with Amma, Savitri's mother whined, saying, 'To hell with all the dreams in the world. Who knows whether they really had such a dream or not? I'm sure they bluffed and ditched my daughter. I don't know why God cursed us humans with these bloody dreams in the first place!'

In her last days, Amma grew very fearful of the dreams she saw. 'Four guys came to take me away,' she'd say, describing the dream and then crying. Banking on the belief that a nightmare wouldn't come true if you slept after that, she'd try hard to catch some post-dream sleep, but in vain. Before going to bed, she'd chant many hymns to make sure that she wouldn't have any dreams in her sleep. To guard her empire of sleep from the invading hordes of dreams, she'd keep a photo of Bhutaraja under her pillow.

But Amma couldn't escape her dreams—or death! The question that cropped up in my mind when I heard the news of Amma's demise was, 'What dream did Amma have prior to her death?'

12

SAVIOUR ORPHAN

2 October 2006

IT HAS BEEN OVER FIFTEEN YEARS SINCE I MOVED TO Bangalore. If a new acquaintance now asks me 'Where are you from?' I go quiet for a minute. As long as the house I was born and raised in was under my family's name, the thread that bound me to my hometown remained intact. But it has been a long time since I sold it off and renovated my Bangalore apartment from its proceeds. Of late, I've slowly started feeling that I have become a Bangalorean. I've started telling people that I'm from Bangalore. But when someone says that they are from Bellary district, I'm delighted and quickly admit that I also hail from the same place.

Selling off one's ancestral home is very painful indeed. I felt like I was sending the cow that had lovingly provided me with milk and sustenance to the butcher. But the hard realities of life always triumph over emotions. If I was to rent it out, the tenants may not have paid me the dues properly. If I left it vacant, it would have fallen apart without regular maintenance. And what if someone started squatting there?

What if they began using it as a hideout to conduct illegal activities?

It's a bitter truth that Bangalore real estate prices make my native house seem like a mere emotional cord resonating only within me. After much brooding, I finally decided to sell it off. I spread the word among my many relatives and friends, and one person expressed interest in buying it. The deal was completed smoothly.

Sorting through the things we'd left behind at our house, Akka and I retained a few items for ourselves and gave away the rest to the needy and the destitute. Although most things were disposed of, we were left with a good number of photos of gods that had adorned our house for years. Having built modern homes where we hesitate to drill even a single nail into the wall, how could we accommodate all those photos? Moreover, flaunting these pictures of gods all over the house was no longer trendy!

I thought of donating it to the nearby temple, and approached the temple priest.

'Many families who lived here for generations are selling their houses and moving to Bangalore. Everyone thinks having these photos spoil the aesthetic appeal of modern houses. If all of them come and dump their photos here, what am I supposed to do with all that junk?' the priest demanded.

Someone suggested that Akka and I place them under a tree in the forest. How could I desert our gods who have protected us all these years in a forest? Moreover, being an eco-friendly person, how could I dump trash in a forest and harm the ecosystem?

Slowly, the problem of these photos was growing larger than I had imagined. It was indeed painful to see Anatha

Rakshaka, the saviour of orphans, who protected us for decades, turn anatha himself—the saviour orphan was being rendered homeless himself!

Both Appa and Amma were very pious and religious people. Once a God came home, even in the form of a calendar, they would remain at home for good. The dates, months and other details were a mere formality. Only the glittering images of gods mattered to them. At the end of the year, they'd get it framed, hit another nail in the wall recklessly and hang the photo there. From the very next day, along with the numerous other photos accumulated over the years, the new one too would be adorned with a tilak. Amma would then wave incense sticks before the photos and take out an aarthi en masse.

Every time my parents went on a pilgrimage, at every temple they'd invariably buy the photos of that particular god. Manjunatha of Dharmasthala, Krishna of Udupi, Tirupati's Timmappa, Manchali's Raghappa, Sannuthi's Chandrala, Hampi's Yanthroddhara, Puri Jagannatha, Kashi Vishwanatha, Badri Narayana, Kolhapura Lakshmi … The list was endless. If this wasn't enough, many friends and relatives returning from pilgrimages also gifted us photos of gods along with the prasadam.

Outside, the space above the entrance door was reserved for the Bhootaraja of Swadi. We slept securely at night, knowing that the many gods adorning the walls would stay awake and protect us. Whenever we committed any mistake, we'd be scared to look these gods in the eye. We basked in their approval when we did good deeds. They never allowed us to feel lonely ever.

There was another set of photos of gods that had nothing to do with any pilgrimage site, but would be required for some specific feasts and poojas. They included Satya Narayana, Vata Savitri, Surya Narayana, Purandara Dasa, Budha Brihaspathi, Vara Mahalakshmi and the like.

Every year, on the full moon day of the Vata Savitri Vratha, after the pooja was over, Amma would read the story of Savitri. Kashavva, the tonsured widow, would come and sit at the entrance door and listen to the story. When the part where Yamadharma throws his noose around the soul of Satyavan and pulls him along would be read out, Kashavva would cry uncontrollably. Despite listening to the same old story every year, she would always cry with the same intensity.

That year wasn't any different. After Amma finished reading the story, Kashavva wiped her eyes with the seragu of her saree and said, 'Look what sort of a pativrathe Savitri must have been! She fought Yama himself to save her husband and thereby saved the five pearls of a married woman to remain a muttaide.'

'Did she sell off all the pearls and become very rich, Kashajji?' I asked, curiously.

'God forbid! Do you even know what you are saying, putta? Only a married woman whose husband is still alive can adorn herself with those five pearls called kumkuma, nose ring, mangalsutra, bangles and the toe ring. No wealth in the world can ever be bigger than that. There's no bigger honour than having those five pearls and being called a muttaide,' said Kashavva, letting out a heavy sigh.

'It is all due to one's karma; what can anyone do but take life as it comes?' said Amma bracingly.

'When my husband passed away, like Savitri, I also had a strong urge to chase Yama, fight with him and bring my husband back to life, you know? But unfortunately, it's beyond mere mortals like us,' conceded Kashavva.

On Purandara Dasa's memorial day, right from the crack of dawn to late in the night, we all would sing Dasara padas and bhajans. Amma and Akka had sweet voices, and sang melodiously. Although I couldn't sing very well, I would actively participate in bhajan singing. Singing in a chorus didn't demand a good voice, it demanded spirit and I had that in good measure. Many of our neighbours would also join us.

Among the photos we had, there was a hand-sketched picture of Hanumantha as well. I had drawn it for a competition in school. It was a picture of Hanuman flying across the ocean, holding his mace in one hand and carrying the sanjeevani in the other. In the picture, his tail had spiralled around his long body and emerged near his head. I had won a consolation prize for that drawing.

Akka always used to make fun of that picture and taunt me, saying, 'Your Hanuman is so undernourished and scrawny; how can anyone so skinny lift a mountain?' she'd ask. 'How can his tail defy the laws of gravity and stiffly look skywards? Should it not be dangling downwards?'

But Amma ignored Akka's banters and got my drawing framed and hung it on the wall with all other gods. Eventually, there came a time when even Akka had to humbly bow down before that picture and worship it!

My parents had looked at quite a few alliances for Akka, but due to one reason or the other, none of those proposals worked out. Appa and Amma were getting anxious, and Akka was starting to get dejected by the rejections. An elderly person told us that Akka would get a suitable groom if she worshipped Lord Hanuman and kept a dot of sandalwood paste on his tail every day. Akka was desperate enough to follow any suggestion if it would get her a good marriage match.

Every day, after performing the pooja, Akka started to adorn the tail in the photo of my drawing with a dot of sandalwood paste. Akka's devotion to Hanumanji soared so high that she could no longer notice his bony body or the illogical, upstanding tail. By the time Hanuman's tail was fully covered by sandal dots, a good alliance was indeed finalized.

Amma soon started singing praises about the power of Hanuman in that photo wherever she went. Influenced by Amma's words, two more girls adorned Hanuman's tail with sandalwood paste dots in a bid to secure a good marriage alliance. Whether it was the power of Lord Hanuman or sheer coincidence, but even those two girls found suitable matrimonial matches soon after completing their vowed pledge.

Following suit, Krishnavenamma made her daughter, Manji, perform the same rituals. But strangely, although the entire tail was covered in sandalwood paste dots, no alliance came through. Fortunately, Krishnavenamma saved Hanuman's grace by saying, 'If my daughter isn't destined to get married in the first place, what can any god do about it?'

We didn't have a photograph of the original idol of Gandi Narasimha Swamy, although he was our family deity. There was a reason for this. The God at the temple was so powerful that no camera could ever capture the image of its idol. Apparently, a stubborn British woman who clandestinely captured the idol's photograph is said to have invited the wrath of the ferocious Lord Narasimha. People say that, within minutes, she vomited blood and died right there. Even today, a picture of that lady on a horseback can be seen in the temple tower.

As though to topple all our beliefs, Gopanna Master's son, Prahlada, came from Bangalore. Prahlada, who was well versed with the sophistications of huge cities, once clicked a photograph of Gandi Narasimha Swamy without anyone's knowledge. He thoroughly enjoyed exposing our fatuousness, and bragged about how he'd captured the image of the original idol and proved everyone wrong.

Appa and Amma were very upset. 'May the vile philanderer that portrayed our God as powerless never prosper in any of his next seven lives,' cursed Amma, angrily. They vowed to never keep a photo of the God in our house as a mark of their loyalty to him.

On the eve of Prahlada's return to Bangalore, Amma invited him over for dinner. The bisibele bhat was too hot and spicy. Just as Prahlada ate the first couple of morsels, his mouth started burning—water started dripping from his eyes and nose. Instead of giving him water, Amma kept saying, 'Apologize for your sins to Lord Narasimha, everything will be alright.'

Besides the photos of gods, we had quite a few photos of our ancestors and elders as well. In one of the photos, our Ajji, drooping under hefty loads of jewellery she was wearing, was standing next to Ajja, dressed in a coat and dhoti, flaunting a walking stick with the head of a roaring lion for a handle. Next to it was the sepia-toned photo of Appa–Amma standing next to each other. Akka–Bhava's colourful honeymoon photo, in which Bhava had posed with his arm around Akka in Ooty's Botanical Gardens, was also there. There was a photo of me as a baby, lying on a rubber sheet and looking curiously into the camera. Akka garlanding PM Indira Gandhi when she'd visited our town; Appa wearing a mortar board and posing with his degree certificate at his convocation; Amma, clad in an 'American' georgette saree and conspicuously flaunting her wristwatch; and Akka's craft work of a swan made of buttons were all there.

There was also a photo of a lady we knew nearly nothing about. Her name was Rindamma, apparently. She had a grim, serious face with large eyes. Appa respected her enormously. But he also didn't know who she was exactly. Right from my Ajja's time, everyone in the family respected her. Everybody believed that the lady had toiled all her life for the welfare of our family. But no one knew where, how or when. On Pitru Paksha, the day we worshipped our ancestors, a pinda would be offered to her without fail.

We also had a group photo taken at the wedding of Appa's second uncle. Appa looked just like me in that photograph. Even at that young age, he was wearing a dhoti, coat and hat. Once, Akka had dressed me up in the same costume for a fancy dress competition at our school. I'd won the first prize that day.

Whenever any elderly relatives visited our house, they'd keep looking at this photo for hours. 'This is Sundaramma, posing before she left for Kashi. Can you believe this is our Anantha? Look at how fat Gundu Kaka used to be!' they'd go on joyfully.

But Appa's Chikkamma, my Chikkajji, hated that snap because she wasn't in it. Barely a year after their wedding, the lady who was sitting next to Chikkappa in the photo had passed away during her first child birth. Chikkajji would grudgingly say, 'My co-wife never ceases to haunt me even after her death.'

Nevertheless, Sarojakka—the child who had survived that difficult birth—would keep looking at the mother she had never seen with wide eyes.

The guy who'd bought our house promptly handed over more than 200 framed photos to me. With every photo, many memories came rushing back. How could I preserve them? The gods and the elders who led us through all the ups and downs of life seemed to beg me to somehow protect them. The nails of Ugra Narasimha had become blunt. The gold coins pouring out of Lakshmi's hands had lost their sheen. The plantain leaf festoons on either side of Lord Satya Narayana had dried up. The Sun God was eclipsed.

After two days of pondering over what I could do, an idea suddenly struck me. I painstakingly took out each photo from their frame, had them scanned and saved the soft copies onto a CD. Inserting my pinkie finger into the hole in the centre of the CD, I lifted my hand and felt thrilled by imagining myself as a modern-day version of Govardhanagiridhari—Lord Krishna lifting the mountain Govardhana. I was carrying our 33 million gods at the tip of my little finger!

Now, all the gods and elders have become the screensaver for my laptop. If I pause working even for a while, one after the other, they start appearing on the screen to give their darshan. Every glimpse of those pictures feels like being on a nostalgic sojourn through my childhood.

13

MORTAL BODIES, IMMORTAL SOULS

7 March 2007

IN OUR TOWN, IT WAS THE KORACHAS WHO PLAYED the band for both auspicious and inauspicious occasions. Whether it was a wedding or a funeral, wherever they were invited, they'd come and play the same instruments with equal commitment. The genre, however, varied significantly. Although they played various songs from newly released films at weddings, for funerals, they stuck to a solitary pathos song. While they'd wear colourful uniforms for weddings, they would wear their regular, daily clothes for funerals.

Incidentally, the Korachas lived right behind our house. No matter who died in town, the funeral procession had to pass by our house. The way to the graveyards of all the castes had to go through our street. Except Brahmins, more or less every other caste who buried their dead, used to have the band set for the funerals and contacted the Korchas. Usually, the corpses of the affluent would have grand processions accompanying them to the graveyard.

Most communities followed the practice of throwing a few coins along with puffed rice over the corpses, while carrying it for burial. Every procession would be followed by a band of poor kids, fighting among themselves to grab as many coins as they could. My classmates were also part of this little band following funeral processions.

If you have travelled by train, I am sure you would have noticed that the railway guard rings the bell three times for every train passing through a station. The first to announce that a train would arrive soon, the second one when they get a confirmation on the train crossing the previous station and finally, the third, when it almost reaches the station. Very much like that, in every funeral, the Korachas played in three distinct spells.

The first spell lasted about ten minutes and was meant to spread the news of the death to the entire town. Invariably, the burials and the processions were carried out in daytime. Maybe it was to allow people to view the departed person one last time clearly in the daylight, or maybe it was because folks feared stepping into graveyards after dusk. Even if someone passed away in the evening, the funeral procession would leave only the following day. The moment people heard the band strike their first note in the morning, everybody would pause whatever they were doing and speculate about who might have kicked the bucket. If it was someone known, they'd immediately rush to the house of the deceased. If it was someone they didn't know so well, they would simply resume their work, saying, 'Someone from the Potter's Lane, it seems,' or 'Looks like someone from the lone Masjid Lane has passed away.'

The second spell of the band lasted about five to ten minutes. It was meant to inform everyone that the corpse was ready for its final journey, and that all the friends and relatives of the deceased had arrived. It could also be construed as the last call for people to come and catch a final glimpse of the corpse at the residence of the deceased.

The third and final spell would begin about fifteen minutes after the conclusion of the second. It meant that the bier was being lifted. This final spell wouldn't stop till the corpse reached the burial ground. As the corpse got closer to our house, the band would get louder and louder, and then fade slowly as it moved away, past our house.

Once the third spell starts, everyone in the streets leading to the graveyard stop what they are doing and come out to the front yard to catch a glimpse of the procession. Kids, babies, pregnant women, new mothers—everyone at home during the day, without any exception would stand in front of their houses. Once, one of our relatives who had come to visit us tried to drive us in, saying, 'All children get inside; you guys shouldn't watch the funeral.'

But we ignored him and stayed right there.

Meanwhile, Amma came to our rescue, saying, 'For all you know, in a small town like ours there'll hardly be one or two funerals or wedding processions every two or three months. How can we restrict the kids from watching even that?'

Even the new mothers would carry the infants on their hips and watch the procession.

It was customary for wedding processions to move slowly. Funeral processions, on the other hand, didn't have any such restrictions and tended to move pretty quickly. However, when the departed hailed from a rich family and the corpse was well-decorated, the funeral processions moved rather slowly. Such processions always avoided shortcuts and reached the graveyard only after covering as many lanes as they could.

The Korachas led the procession, playing their band. The menfolk followed the Korachas with the bier following them. In the end, the women would trail. Except Brahmins, women from all other castes would go to the graveyards with the procession. The folks in the procession consciously avoided directly looking at the onlookers watching them.

Once people saw the corpse, they'd identify who had passed away. As it was a small town, more or less everybody knew everybody else, at least by face. Looking at the corpse, people would say, 'He's the guy who operated the dry chilli pounding machine in the mill at Gouler's Lane,' or 'She's the one who'd come as Jogamma every Tuesday and Friday. She'd generously give bhandara, turmeric powder, to everyone,' or 'This guy used to drive the lorry for the mines, a chronic drunkard, it seems.'

After the procession passed, people would air their views about it, saying, 'The colour of the saree they'd draped on the corpse was very nice,' or 'Did you notice that despite losing his wife, the blackguard didn't have a trace of tears in his eyes? The men, by and large, are stone-hearted, I tell you,' or 'Despite four guys holding her back, she was crying so uncontrollably. Nothing can match the grief of a mother, you know.'

If someone travelling into our town accidentally ran into the funeral procession, it was regarded as a good omen for them. If people going out for any important work knew beforehand that there would be a funeral procession, they'd deliberately time their departure to confront the corpse face to face. People seeking marriage alliances for their children were sure to strike good matches if they saw a corpse on their way.

On the contrary, the sight of people returning from the graveyard after burying the corpse was regarded as a bad omen. Everybody avoided seeing them. The very folks who had come to see them on their journey to the graveyard with the corpse and the band would avoid them like the plague on their way back.

Whenever there was a funeral in town, after dusk, Shanthappa would invariably come to our house for a chat with Amma. In our town, across castes, Shanthappa was usually the man who decked up the corpses for the procession. Drinking the coffee Amma gave him, and taking betel leaves and nuts from her, he'd ask with pride, 'How was the decoration today, Amma?'

He'd feel satisfied only when Amma praised him, saying his work was very good. But Amma was stingy with her praise. 'Again you draped the corpse with the same old red saree, Shanthappa! Really, I'm so used to seeing corpses in a red saree nowadays that someday I'm afraid I'll mistake a living person wearing a red saree for a corpse!' she'd complain.

'What can I do, Amma? That weaver Vamanna sold me a dozen red sarees in one go, for a pittance. By mistake, he missed a few strands while weaving them, it seems. As I knew that the corpses wouldn't complain, I thought it was a deal I shouldn't refuse. Now, I don't have a choice but to use them till I exhaust that stock,' Shanthappa would explain his predicament.

'And the face also had turned all black,' Amma would crib.

'You tell me, what could I do, Amma! The woman had passed away last evening itself. Her skin had turned so pale that no amount of snow or powder could brighten it up,' he'd justify.

After keeping him on tenterhooks for a while, Amma would finally say, 'Anyway, on the whole, it wasn't so bad. In fact, it was rather good from a distance. And no one would look too closely at a corpse, would they? I think it almost looked like a live person only.'

Hearing those compliments from Amma, Shanthappa would leave with a triumphant smile on his face.

Ambanna was the chief of the Koracha band. He'd visit us daily at 7.45 a.m. and at 1.30 p.m. That was when Dharwad Radio Station would broadcast film songs. In our house, we had an enormous radio, as big as a TV, with glowing lights. Every day, Ambanna would sit on the parapet of our house and listen to all the songs on the radio.

A true artist, Ambanna wanted to always enhance his repertoire. He paid special attention to new songs and would try to learn them as quickly as he could. We could hear him diligently practising the new songs he'd heard on the radio the previous day. That's how he added a few special attractions for every wedding season. He'd pick only peppy numbers with fast beats and avoid the slower ones. 'Who will ever like a tune that you can't dance to?' he'd reason.

He neither understood nor was bothered about the lyrics of the song. According to him, a fast-paced spiritual song of renunciation like *'Kuladalli Keelyavudo hucchappa'* worked just fine for wedding processions. People didn't seem to mind as they passionately danced to its tune. However, there was no such confusion when it came to funeral processions. The band conveniently played the same melancholic dirge for every death.

Early one morning, we all heard the funeral song being played quite close by and started trying to guess who could have died in our neighbourhood. After listening attentively for some time, the tune could be traced back to Ambanna's house. Everyone wondered who could have died there! Amma asked me to run across and bring Ambanna along. He immediately came with me.

'Why are you playing that ghastly tune early in the morning when no one has died?' Amma enquired.

'I'm training Hanumanthu, Amma. Nowadays, my cough is getting worse and worse. Can't say how long I'll be able to play my pipe,' he said. Hanumanthu was Ambanna's son and Akka's classmate.

'To hell with your training. First thing in the morning, if I listen to that terrible dirge, my heart skips a beat. You can't just teach your son these awful tunes anywhere you want!' said Amma, sternly.

'Where else can I go, Amma?' Ambanna argued.

After brooding over the matter for a while, Amma came up with a suggestion. 'Go and teach him the dirge at the Gandi Narasimha Swamy Temple. Anyway, God doesn't care whether it's a wedding song or a funeral song. For Lord

Narasimha, a hymn and a dirge are one and the same. In fact, isn't he the one who's playing them both in everyone's lives?'

Amma's spiritual angle was what eventually convinced Ambanna. He started training Hanumanthu on the bank of the rivulet next to the Gandi Narasimha Swamy Temple. As the funeral tune wasn't as intricate as wedding tunes, Ambanna had chosen to start his son's training with the dirge.

Hanumanthu didn't have to wait too long to make his public debut. The opportunity was provided by the washerwoman, Kallavva, on a day when Ambanna's cough was particularly aggravated. Hanumanthu, being a novice, was naturally nervous. Ambanna walked along with him for moral support. Quite unsure whether he would win folks' approval, Hanumanthu tentatively started playing the pipe. As he entered our lane, he got even more nervous. He was conscious of Akka, his classmate, standing at the entrance of our house and evaluating his performance. His hands and legs were trembling slightly. As he passed the house, he looked at Akka from the corner of his eye. She joined the tips of her thumb and index finger and formed a circle to show her appreciation. Hanumanthu understood that she was indicating that he was doing well.

Egged on by Akka, Hanumanthu started to really rock it, very spiritedly. People genuinely praised him for his splendid debut that day. In the coming days, people started to specifically demand for Hanumanthu to play at the funerals of their family members. Being a quick learner, he also soon added many peppy film songs to his repertoire, and extended his popularity to weddings and other auspicious functions as well.

Gradually, Ambanna got sidelined. In a couple of years, he actually had to beg Hanumanthu for even fifty paise to buy beedis.

If someone we don't know very well passes away, we may feel curious or perplexed, or even a little scared. But the real pain of death hits us hard only when we lose our dear ones. I experienced it when I lost Appa. So to speak, Appa's death wasn't totally unexpected. He was quite old and had mellowed down considerably. Every night after dinner, while taking their tablets, Appa–Amma would endlessly speculate who'd be the first to go. But on that day, when the three of us were having dinner, a grain of rice accidentally entered Appa's windpipe and he started struggling to breathe. Amma was asking him to drink some water, and I was urging him to try coughing so that the rice could come out. But Appa did neither, and instead his eyes rolled upwards.

Amma realized what happened and started yelling, 'Gone, gone … Narayana, Narayana, Narayana.'

When I realized that I was holding Appa's corpse, I experienced a sudden fear—I was shivering and in pain.

Later, once she had calmed down a little, Amma said, 'Let's not cremate him in this unknown city like an orphan. Let's take him to our town.'

I agreed. So, I booked an Ambassador car for the trip. The driver asked for double the fare for transporting a corpse. My landlord, who was quite friendly with our family, volunteered to come with us. Struck with grief, Amma took solace in doing small tasks—she cleared the table and cleaned the kitchen.

I didn't know where to lay Appa in the car.

'Let's just tie up the body with a rope and shove it inside the boot, sir,' the driver said, quite matter-of-factly.

I was shocked to hear that! 'No way! I can't just put Appa in the boot,' I protested, teary-eyed.

'That's how they transport corpses, putta,' Amma said quietly.

I couldn't agree and called an ambulance instead. They asked for three thousand rupees more. I readily agreed and booked it, and told them that we wanted to start early in the morning. The ambulance had enough space to lay Appa down, and Amma and I could sit next to him. The landlord sat in the passenger seat next to the driver.

By the time we crossed Hiriyur, it was already 2 p.m. The driver stopped the ambulance at a hotel for coffee. The landlord came to me and said, 'Look, your mother is diabetic. She hasn't had anything to eat since morning. Somehow convince her to eat something. It'll be evening by the time we'll be done with the cremation. It's not good for her to fast till then. And you should also eat something.'

I had a couple of idlis. However, it was hard to convince Amma.

'How can I eat at a time like this? No, I just can't,' Amma refused.

I reminded her how she had to be hospitalized a couple of times, as her diabetes had aggravated after her fasting.

She then held out an idli towards Appa, and said, 'Please don't think otherwise. Although I hate eating at a time like this, you know how adamant putta is. Saying this, she reluctantly ate a couple of idlis.

After a while, Amma dozed off. When the ambulance ran over a road bump, she suddenly jolted back awake and apologetically slapped her own cheeks a couple of times for falling asleep next to her departed soulmate.

As Appa had lived in our town all his life, quite a few people had come to pay their last respects. There was a lot of buzz due to all the crying and the talk about Appa's life. Suddenly, a local politician for whom Appa had worked for a long time arrived to pay his condolences. People started chatting about his arrival in whispers. A pin-drop silence prevailed over the place. Even Amma bent her head and turned silent. The leader bowed down before Appa's body, spoke a few comforting words to no one in particular and left. The buzz returned after his exit. All of us resumed grieving.

Meanwhile, Gopanna Master, my old teacher, called me aside and said, 'Quickly take a bath at the well and drape yourself with this dhoti. We need to finish the cremation before it gets dark.' He then handed me a dhoti and said, 'I bought an expensive one thinking that it could be used later as well.' He then went out to oversee the work of preparing the bier.

I was alone in the backyard. I started drawing water from the well. As I was drawing the third pot of water, I sensed that someone was standing near the back door of the house. I drew the pot up, placed it on the low wall of the well and turned around. I was surprised to see Amma standing there. I couldn't fathom Amma moving away from Appa's body and coming here.

She came closer to me and said gently, 'Graveyards can be scary. You are still young. But don't be scared. After lighting up the pyre, stand away from it. Sometimes the skull bursts loudly.'

I nodded my head. She went back to sit with Appa.

Although Ambanna, Hanumanthu and Shanthappa had come, they had no role to play, as there's no decoration or band for a Brahmin funeral. The priest and the elders poured two brass pots of water, stripped Appa's body and draped it in a white cloth. Tying the corpse to the bamboo bier, circumambulating in an anticlockwise direction, and putting sesame and water into the corpse's mouth, they lifted the bier saying, 'Narayana ... Narayana ...' and headed towards the graveyards. I was asked to walk ahead carrying some lit coal in a clay pot.

'Don't turn around and see who is following you,' Gopanna Master instructed.

This is embarrassing, but I have to share it here. As we all briskly walked past the Eshwara temple, I had a sudden urge to defecate. In the sudden shock of Appa's demise and the hurry of transporting Appa's remains in the ambulance, I had totally forgotten to ease myself.

'No, not at an hour like this. Such trivial matters cannot bother me when I am suffering such grave grief,' I told myself and continued to walk.

Breathing deeply, I repeatedly told myself that all was well and moved on. But by the time we reached Bhairappa's temple, the pressure had become unbearable. Unable to walk any further, I just stopped. Gopanna Master came up to me to check why I had stopped. I shared my predicament with him and said, 'I'll just hop into Paddakka's house on the next street, be done with it and come back.'

'You won't be allowed inside any house now, putta,' he told me. 'Don't you know there's a ten-day sutaka for the family members of the deceased?'

'I'll quickly go to our house only.'

'You can't do all that, my boy. Somehow bear it till we reach graveyard,' Gopanna Master pleaded.

But how could I?

'What happened?' the guys carrying Appa's bier asked.

'Oh, nothing …' replied Gopanna Master.

'The corpse is heavy; keep moving quickly and don't pause in between,' urged someone impatiently.

I started walking briskly. At that moment, I wasn't thinking about Appa's death or Amma's grief. All I wanted was to ease myself. The moment we reached the graveyard, I placed the pot on the ground and ran towards the water pit. Once relieved, I had no option but to wash myself in the muddy waters of that fly-infested fungal pit itself. When I returned, everyone, including Appa, was waiting for me. I felt sorry and embarrassed.

The day after the cremation, people started coming home to meet Amma. Everyone had to be briefed about the when, where, how and why of Appa's demise. Amma had to cry before every new visitor. By the seventh day, I was fed up with the whole thing and desperately wished for normalcy to return to our lives at the earliest.

One day, three women from Hospet came to meet Amma. Although Amma knew all three of them very well, one of them, Vaidehi, had created quite a buzz recently.

Vaidehi used to sit at the cash counter of their grocery store to assist her husband. Apparently, about a couple of months ago, she had fallen in love with a Malayali boy who used to visit their shop for the pigmy collection and had eloped with him. Her devastated husband was said to have grieved a lot for his missing wife.

Naturally, everyone in our house was looking at Vaidehi very curiously. After the customary enquiries and after Amma shed copious tears, the visitors placated her, and I (as usual), described the circumstances and details of Appa's demise. Meanwhile, Vaidehi went to the backyard to wash her legs.

Barely had she disappeared behind the back door, when Amma furiously whispered, 'When did she come back?'

'Last week,' they replied, in an equally hushed tone.

'Did her husband accept her despite her betrayal?' Amma probed deeper.

'Henpecked bastard, accepted without a whimper. He was finding it hard to cook for himself and take care of the shop, it seems,' one of them said, contemptuously.

'She's said to have convinced her husband, saying that she hadn't run away wantonly, and the Malayali bastard had cast an occult spell on her and all that,' added the other.

By then some visitors arrived from Bellary. Once again, everyone took on the roles prescribed—the visitors enquiring and Amma crying.

I was quite devastated by the happenings of the last few days. But listening to Amma's gossip gave me some solace that life would, after all, come back on track like before. It was just a matter of time.

14

VARAAHA PRIYA: THE PIG LOVER

13 April 2007

THE VERSES BELOW ARE THE OPENING LINES OF A popular composition of Sri Purandara Dasa.

Nindakarirabeku Jagadolu Nindakarirabeku,
Handi iddare keri hyange shuddhavo haange,
Andandu maadida papavemba mala tindu hoguvaraiah,
Nindakarirabeku Jagadolu Nindakarirabeku,
Nindakarirabeku Jagadolu Nindakarirabeku

The world needs slanderous men.
Akin to the pigs that keep the lanes clean,
Slandering cleans up the daily sins we commit.
Just the way pigs eat up the filth we shit,
The world needs slanderous men.
The world needs slanderous men

Although Saint Purandara Dasa is primarily speaking about the slanderers here, I find his words about the pigs more interesting. True, one has to accept that, to some extent, pigs do clean up the filth in the lanes they frequent, but it's perhaps more true that pigs hardly enter a lane that's already clean. As all the towns of Bellary district are devoid of basic underground drainage, every lane there is a safe haven for pigs.

Ours is a town where droves of pigs thrive—the sewage has nowhere to flow and pools along the side of the road. Here, kids squat in a row and take a dump. One can find plantain and hand-stitched palash leaves thrown away with leftover food and peeled fruit skins buzzing with flies casually thrown in the middle of the road, the uncleanable 100×100 trash pits and so on. It's hard to imagine a lane or town in Uttara Karnataka being free of pigs. The fact that Purandara Dasa has mentioned pigs at a time when pearls and gems were being traded on roadsides in the Vijayanagara empire speaks volumes about the historical legacy of these pigs.

Compared to many other animals, pigs are harmless creatures. They don't bark or bite like dogs, nor do they snatch away things like monkeys. They don't sneak into our kitchens to drink up all the milk stealthily, and they don't even bite us like mosquitoes, ants or bedbugs. These poor souls live by themselves, consuming the waste thrown away so carelessly by society. Yet, society doesn't really treat them with respect. They don't get pampered like cats and dogs. They don't get attention like mischievous monkeys do. They can't sneak inside homes, like mosquitoes, ants or bedbugs. The moment pigs are sighted, people shoo them away with contempt.

Kashavva used to tell us a story about the slimy pigs in our town. Once upon a time, there used to be a great saint in our town. He apparently had a big team of disciples who respected him a lot. The omniscient mystique was believed to have had knowledge of the past, present and future. Hence, the saint was aware of the fact that, in his next life, he'd be reborn as a pig in our town itself.

Naturally, the saint was very upset at the prospect of being born as a filthy pig. So, one day he summoned all his disciples and informed them about his impending life as a pig. He added that even as a pig his disciples would be able to easily identify him in his next life, as he'd have a white stripe over his forehead. He instructed them to not only identify him in pig form, but also kill that pig without any mercy. He assured them that they didn't have to hesitate to relieve him from that misery, as he would loathe living in the gutters as a swine. He also reassured them that by killing him in his next life, they'd be paying their oblations to him and cautioned them that learning wouldn't come in handy if they didn't pay their Guru Dakshina.

In a couple of years, the saint passed away. His devout disciples started diligently scouting for their guru in the puddles, pits, gutters and sewers of the town. Although they couldn't find the saint for quite a while, they kept searching relentlessly. After about two years, they finally spotted a pig with a white stripe frolicking in the slimy gutters. It didn't take too long for the smart protégés of the great guru to identify their master. In single-minded pursuit of offering the Guru Dakshina to their beloved Guru, throwing away any moral conflicts they may have felt to the wind, the disciples set out to slay the animal, wielding swords and daggers.

In the blazing afternoon sun, the Guru was gleefully chilling in the stinking silt of a sewer. After paying their respects to him, just as they lifted their weapons to strike, 'Just stop!' yelled the pig, in the voice of their Guru.

'Please don't kill me. I had no clue how cosy the life of a swine could be! It's a thousand times better than the life of humans. I urge you all to start your penance right away for being blessed to be born as pigs in your next life,' said the Guru.

Bewildered by the sudden turn of events, the disciples returned home.

In the end, Kashavva would conclude by saying, 'So the moral of the story is: Appearances can be deceptive; you have to really experience things before you make any judgements.'

Despite the fact that pigs are generally stigmatized, the people of Bellary have a strange belief that pigs are a form of Goddess Lakshmi. I guess the emperors of the Vijayanagara empire are responsible for it. Besides making the pig their royal insignia, they also had its emblem etched on the gold coins they minted. Drawing from the term 'varaaha', the pig, those coins came to be known as varahas.

The science of dream interpretation also endorses that the appearance of pigs in dreams signifies the prospect of getting wealthy. There's an even stranger belief that if a pig accidentally enters a house, and is killed and buried in the hallway of the house, it'll turn into gold! Readers may recall that the renowned Kannada author KumVee has written a wonderful story based on such a belief.

Amma also strongly believed that a pig buried in the hallway would turn into gold. With conviction, she'd say, 'When I came to this town as a newlywed, that Shetty family in the Kalamma Lane couldn't even afford two square meals a day. How do you think they're able to live like royalty now? A few years ago, a hefty pig rushed into their house by chance. They promptly killed it and buried its body in their hallway. Now, whenever they need money, all they do is dig where they buried the pig, cut a piece of the pig's ear or tail, or even pluck a couple of its teeth.' In a hushed tone, she further revealed, 'Do you know the heavy jewellery the women of the family flaunt comes from the swine's tongue, intestine or a limb?'

Every day, she wished and waited for a healthy pig to barge into our house.

And that day did arrive!

One day, a large pig rushed into our house!

It was my grandfather's death anniversary. Amma had woken up early and had tidily prepared vada, payasam, rasam, yellunde, rice and all the other foods ceremonially prepared on the day of a vaideeka. After taking a bath at the well, Appa wore his sacred thread, the yajnopavita, to the left, donned a twisted dry-hay ring called pavithram on his ring finger and washed the feet of the priest. Amma served all the delicacies to the priest on a plantain leaf spread out on the floor. On such death anniversaries, everybody else was supposed to eat only after the priest finished his meal. With drooling lips and gluttonous eyes, Akka and I kept surveying the assorted food placed on the plantain leaf. Appa reverentially folded his hands, uttered 'Govinda', and poured an uddharane of water on the mound of rice.

Suddenly, making a gurgling noise, the pig rushed in from the back door and directly attacked the food on the leaf. God knows where that monster of a pig was hiding. None of our shouting was of any use. Within no time, it swallowed everything, including the leaf. I'm sure no one familiar with the taste of Amma's delicious cooking would blame the poor pig for what it did.

Despite all the chaos, Amma didn't lose her golden focus and yelled to Appa, 'Catch it right away. Fortunately, Lakshmi herself has arrived home. Don't let go of it, it's literally worth its weight in gold ... Catch it, catch it ... Don't let it leave!'

But Appa was too terrified to even move an inch. Having had a sumptuous banquet, the boar walked out of the front door with a royal gait.

Amma immediately started shouting, 'How could you let go of such a golden opportunity? If only you could muster up a little courage!'

'Appa quickly recovered his wits and shot back. Am I not in the consecrated attire? When I'm performing holy rituals in a sanctified state, how could I even touch a pig, of all creatures?'

'So what? You could always pour a potful of water on yourself and do the achamana to purify yourself,' Amma said, sadly.

Unable to fathom his hosts ignoring his situation completely, the priest kept gaping at Amma and Appa helplessly. Akka and I, however, were thrilled to witness this once-in-a-lifetime experience.

In the evening, when all of us were having a chat sitting in the verandah, Amma suddenly sat up, and said, 'Wait a minute ... What if it was my father-in-law who'd arrived in the form of a pig? Isn't it possible that he'd chosen to personally enjoy the meal offered to him by assuming the form of a pig?'

Appa was annoyed by Amma's preposterous words. 'Don't be stupid. My father used to worship Narasimha Saligrama, you know? If at all he came to eat the offerings, he'd rather come in the form of a lion rather than a pig,' Appa retorted, evidently proud of his lineage.

But Amma dismissively said, 'Thankfully, he came as a pig, and ate only the food and the plantain leaf. Had he come as a lion, he would have swallowed the priest as well. For that matter, how is a swine inferior to a lion? After all, both are God's own creation, right?'

Amma never forgot that incident. Like every household, we also faced financial problems: paying my college fees, Akka's wedding expenses, unexpected house repairs and whatnot. In such situations, whenever Appa would struggle to make ends meet, with moist eyes, she'd say, 'If only you'd caught that pig the other day, we wouldn't have any of these hardships, would we?'

Once I finished my engineering degree and landed a software job, our financial woes ended. Within five years, I bought a house in a prestigious apartment colony in Bangalore. I hired a high-end interior decorator and furnished the house with all kinds of novelties like branded bathware, fancy commodes, showers, bathtubs, a state-of-the-art Italian kitchen and whatnot! Appa–Amma were awestruck and would wander through the apartment, touching all the sophisticated gizmos with wide eyes.

Sitting in the second-floor apartment, caressing the glossy marble floor, Amma said, 'There are hardly any pigs in this city. Even if a pig did enter the house by chance, there's no floor under which we can bury it. Yet, Goddess Lakshmi has generously blessed you with all this wealth.'

Ugadi is celebrated with great grandeur in our town. During Ugadi, worshipping the local diety, Basavanna (the Bull God, who is the vahana of Lord Shiva) is a major ritual for us. Starting from the old police station, all the way up to the Virakta Mutt, men would take turns to pull the Basavanna cart in a procession. All the townsfolk would generously throw bananas at the cart. All the streets along the path of the procession would be filled with bananas. The town's pigs that satisfy themselves with mere banana skins all through the year get to feast on a generous supply of full bananas during Ugadi. Droves of pigs follow the procession and clean the streets to the best of their abilities.

The day after Ugadi is Hosa-todaku, marking the start of the new year. On Hosa-todaku, a few spirited youngsters would run all over the town, trying to capture a pig. In order to identify which family a particular pig belonged to, right when they are born, folks would create a permanent scar on them by either slitting their ear or cutting their tail. If I bragged with my friends about Amma making holige for the feast, some of them would show me a pig and boast that their mothers would make pork chops with it the following day.

It would take three to four sturdy youths to catch one big fat pig. Once they identify the pig that belongs to them, two of them will stand at one end of the midden with a large net in their hands. The other two will start chasing the pig from the other end. Sensing that a trap has been laid out to catch it, the petrified pig will start screaming its heart out and run here and there haphazardly. Guarding it from running in other directions, the two chasers keep directing it towards the guys with the net. As it gets closer, the guys holding the net will swing it over the pig and capture the animal. Swinging the net is a skill that demands proper timing and dexterity. If there's even the slightest goof up, the pig will escape. A strong and terrified pig may even attack humans ferociously.

Caught in the net, the pig writhes, wriggles, squeaks and whines. The youths tie up its legs and bind its snout to control the wailing. Then they hang their hunt upside down from a long bamboo pole, do a victory lap around town and carry their catch home. Usually, such a sight invoked both sympathy and admiration—while people genuinely empathized with the pain and grief of the animal, they would also admire the valour of the youth.

'Will they slay it, Appa?' I once asked nervously.

'Pigs die hard. Despite being hit hard continuously, they still don't die that easily. Once a pig is fully beaten down, they throw it onto the spit to roast it,' he said.

I felt distressed listening to this. 'Isn't it wrong to eat a pig, Appa?' I asked.

'It's their way. I don't see anything wrong in it,' Appa said nonchalantly.

There was a special connection between our family deity and pigs.

Ambanna would suddenly show up at our house with a small parcel of palash leaves, and shout from the front yard, 'Anna, are you home?'

Appa would come out. Ambanna would slowly open the parcel of palash leaves. It would contain a bunch of pig hair.

'It should be of the wild boar only, it can't be of the urban pigs,' Appa would say.

'Of course ... Of course, I've personally plucked them from the wild boar only. We went hunting yesterday,' Ambanna would say, sniggering.

'You plucked the hair before killing him, right?'

'Of course ... of course, don't I know how you want them, Anna? I plucked them when he was very much alive and kicking,' Ambanna would swear, placing his palm on his chest.

Appa would cleanse the hair by sprinkling holy water on them and pay two rupees to Ambanna. Thanking Appa profusely, Ambanna would leave for the toddy shop. After that, Appa would meticulously tie all the pig hair together with a metal string and prepare a brush. Such a brush is known as 'Varaaha Kesara'. Appa used Varaaha Kesara to clean all the idols of important gods at our house. But I always suspected that Ambanna wasn't giving Appa wild boar hair.

Once, the day after Ambanna had brought another bunch for Appa, I was curious to know the truth and asked Hanumanthu, Ambanna's son, if his father had gone to hunt a wild boar the previous day. Listening to his reply, I decided to never tell Appa what he had told me.

15

COUNT YOUR BLESSINGS

26 March 2007

OUR NATIONAL POET, RASHTRAKAVI KUVEMPU, once said, 'This sunshine isn't just heat, it's God's blessings.'

I don't know in what sense he said these words. Regardless of what he meant, it's hard for the people of Bellary to say something like this. At the stroke of twelve noon in the month of April, such words sound like a death knell in our part of the country. Only those wishing for a sunstroke would venture out in the open. The whole body feels like a dried-out piece of firewood, so much so that one fears getting charred into ashes at the slightest ignition.

But if you think we get cowed down by such blazing heat, you are grossly mistaken. Toddlers play barefoot in that scorching warmth. Weddings take place in magnificent grandeur and with joy, with scant regard for the blazing sun. People watch kabbadi matches in jam-packed stadiums, relishing hot and spicy puffed rice with green chilli fritters.

This was one of many reasons for Amma to look down upon Bangalore. The first time she visited, she enthusiastically cleaned the puffed rice, sliced grey pumpkins finely and ground chillies. Mixing all these ingredients in the right measure, she prepared the dough to make sandige—a fried snack. However, because Bangalore doesn't see a particularly warm sun, the sandige became hard. When she tried to deep fry them, instead of emerging fluffy and crisp, they just turned black.

Amma's sandige always turned out legendary—and here these were. She was very upset. After she returned home, when her friend Paddakka asked her how she liked Bangalore, Amma said, 'What a wretched city. There's hardly any sun to dry out even happala-sandige, can you believe it? Say what you will, but there's no place like Bellary in the whole world. We get such a blazing sun absolutely free. One should be lucky to be born here.'

Inspired by the blazing sun, Amma prepared the sandige again. This time, the moment they were put into hot oil, they bloomed like marigold flowers. Amma served me the contrasting Bangalore and Bellary sandige in a single plate and proudly said, 'Meet your scraggy Laurel from Bangalore and my bloated Hardy from Bellary. Simply accept the supremacy of Bellary and stop bragging about Bangalore all the time.'

I knew that Amma hated my attitude of praising Bangalore all the time and looked at me as a traitor who'd betrayed Bellary.

Although I have the ability to endure extreme heat, I can barely handle the rains. There are many Kannada stories and poems that celebrate the rains and the rainy season. They seem strange and alien to me; I can't relate to them. In my childhood, I had hardly seen any rain that drenched our parched earth properly. In our town, rains are scarce. In fact, I don't think I had ever seen it rain for more than thirty minutes at a stretch. But I once witnessed the deadly dance of devastating rains when I was in Kolkata (previously Calcutta).

I'd been transferred to Kolkata with a few of my colleagues-turned-friends. All of us used to stay in a common rented house. There was a lake right behind the house. The owner of the house would bathe in that lake daily.

One night, it rained cats and dogs, without any respite. It was so intense that it felt as though the rain gods had poured out the whole Hooghly river over the city in a single night. The lightning and thunder kept startling me every now and then. Since there was a power cut, it was pitch dark. Lying on the bed, I kept on changing sides as I tried to catch some sleep in vain. Every lightning strike seemed to trigger a different image in my mind.

Finally, by dawn, the rain petered out. I drowsily got up and slowly opened the main door. The house was flooded! The lake, the backyard and the roads outside had merged into one. I screamed so loudly that all my friends also woke up and came running out to see what had happened. As I'd opened the door, some water started rushing into the house as well. I started shivering. The film *Bhootayyana Maga Ayyu* came to my mind. In the land of Bengali and Hindi films, I couldn't expect 'Sahasasimha' Vishnuvardhan to rescue me.

I ran up to the first floor, and started banging on the doors of the house owners. I shouted, 'Please come out quickly.

The whole house is waterlogged. Water is rushing inside the house as well.'

'Coming … just five minutes,' the owner replied.

All of us had become very anxious. Moreover, there was this delivery deadline for our new software to a particularly difficult client at the office that day. Not knowing how we'd reach the office in that flood, we were all quite worried.

The landlord couple slowly came down. The wife was carrying an aarthi tray with haldi, kumkum, flowers and camphor. Standing at the main door, she worshipped the water and the threshold of the house. She sang a sweet Bengali song as she sprinkled haldi, kumkum and flowers on the water. She said that Ganga Ma had blessed us by visiting the very doorstep of the house and happily distributed prasad to all of us.

Then, the house owner gave all of us a nylon thread. Just as we were wondering what to do with it, he said, 'Plenty of fish would have arrived with the water last night; come on, start fishing.' He then threw the nylon thread into the water, quickly demonstrating how to catch a fish. 'You guys can enjoy fishing all day. I'll ask my wife to make good fish curry for all of us,' he said, genially.

'We have to go to work! There's a new software we need to deliver urgently,' I stuttered, the nylon thread limp in my hand.

'Why do you even mention your wretched work on a day when we have had such wonderful showers, beta? Enjoy the rains happily. Anyway, the phone lines are down. Nobody will be able to spoil your fun,' the wife advised.

My friends had already thrown their threads in and were enjoying fishing. When I looked around, a lot of people had come outside, and were happily fishing and celebrating the rains.

Even though I had some familiarity with the heat, wind and rains, snow was altogether unknown to me. True, I'd caught a glimpse of snow in the occasional English film, but it had always seemed like a legend from some dreamland. I got to witness it first-hand when I visited England for the first time. I didn't even realized that it had been snowing all through the night. Snowfall doesn't make any noise, unlike rain. It's a silent angel. Occasionally, a silent giantess.

When I opened the back door in the morning, I was awestruck for a minute. It was spotless white everywhere, as though someone had spilled cotton. On the ground, on the cars, on the plants and even on the birds perching on trees, on the sky above the bird ... It was white all over. Just white, white and more white ... I could see no other colour.

I gingerly stepped out of the house and tentatively picked up a fistful of snow. I felt exhilarated. Though it was a Sunday, not daring to go out, I sat in the living room and spent the rest of my day simply gazing at the snow in the backyard.

The next day, the sun came out. Although the tender sunlight wasn't intense enough to melt away the snow, it was bright enough to turn snow into ice. Now, ice on the streets and pavements can be quite dangerous. One is prone to slip and fall if not careful while walking on it.

As my office was close by, I usually walked to work. To keep myself warm, before wearing a thick sweater, I wore two shirts over my thermals. Covering my neck with a woollen scarf and donning a fleece cap, I headed to my office—so disguised that even my Amma wouldn't recognize me. Dressing up in layers to get through the English winter reminded me of an enactment of Mahabharat that I once saw, wherein the person playing Draupadi had draped layer upon layer of sarees for the Vastrapaharanam scene, in which Duryodhana orders Dushasana to strip her.

There was a skywalk on the way to my office. It had been built to help people to cross the gigantic highway that passed beneath. As I started walking on it, I noticed an old lady had slipped and fallen there. Unable to get up on her own, she was lying there, quite helplessly, in that biting cold. I went up to her and helped her stand up.

'Will you please walk me to my daughter's house?' she pleaded.

I agreed. 'Do you want me to call her in the meantime?' I asked, taking out my mobile phone.

'Please don't. My daughter never lets me get out of the house when there's a snowfall,' she said.

Holding her hand, I walked her to her daughter's house.

When I was taking my leave, she gently kissed me on my forehead and blessed me, saying, 'May God bless you, young man.'

'These snowfalls bother you a lot, don't they?' I asked.

'Of course not. Why would they bother me? On the contrary, I wait for these snowfalls all through the year, you know? My husband used to just love snow. He'd make love to me right on the snow, lying in our backyard. Even now, the very thought of the two of us rolling over the snow naked, warms me up, despite the cold,' she blushed.

I laughed heartily.

'Look at that!' she said, excited.

I looked in the direction her finger pointed.

There was a huge pond. All the water had frozen into ice. About half a dozen kids dressed in thin shorts and shirts were skating cheerfully on the ice. Even as they were skating, they scooped up bits of snow lying scattered on the ice, rolled it into little snowballs and kept throwing them at one another.

Watching those kids play with snow, despite the bone-chilling cold, reminded me of my childhood when we used to play lagori barefoot under the formidably hot sun. However, from where I stood, I missed seeing a school of fish play underwater tiggy-tips under the thick, frozen ice!

16

A CELEBRATION CALLED AMMA

2 May 2012

AMMA'S SENSE OF HUMOUR WAS QUITE SPECIAL, IF A little weird. But she'd never concede that she was joking. She'd argue that it was just an apt response in a specific context. She'd never laugh at her own jokes. As she never feared anything or anyone, if she suddenly said something when it was least expected, we didn't know whether to laugh or not. Now when I recall these episodes, I find myself in splits. They bring me so much joy when I think of her that I decided to write down some episodes where Amma's humour shone through.

Once, a newlywed couple moved into the house opposite ours. Both the husband and wife were government employees, and they had been transferred to our town. They did everything in their power to portray themselves as very modern. In about a year, the couple had a baby girl. Like most small-town neighbours, we were curious to know what they were naming their child and enquired about it. But the couple refused to reveal the name.

'It's going to be a surprise!' said the husband.

'We'll disclose it only on the day of the naming ceremony. Until then, keep guessing Ta-da,' added the wife, coyly.

We were a bit perplexed by the way they were creating hype over practically nothing. People in our town usually had no qualms about sharing the baby's proposed name with their relatives and friends well before namakarana. But this couple seemed determined to keep us all in suspense like a Hitchcock thriller.

Meanwhile, we could also see the couple bring home voluminous books of baby names and excitedly search through them. Finally, the day of the naming ceremony arrived. Amma was also invited for it. After handing over the gift and receiving the sweets, kumkum and blouse piece, Amma asked 'So, are you finally ready to divulge the secret? Tell me, what name did you choose eventually?'

'It's modern and yet ancient, you know? I'm sure it's beyond anybody's guess! Her name would be Sudeshna,' declared the baby's mother.

'We picked it from the Mahabharata. It's the name of Virata Raja's wife, you know?' her husband added, proudly.

Amma, being an expert on the Puranas, didn't need any explanations. 'You've chosen a great name indeed. Congratulations! God willing, next year you'll be fathering a Keechaka,' said Amma smoothly, and came home.

In the Mahabharata, Keechaka is Sudeshna's younger brother, who attempted to molest Draupadi! The couple got extremely worried after listening to Amma's take on their baby's name. From the very next day, they started telling people that they had changed the baby's name to 'Sudha'!

'The poor couple had decided on a modern and stylish name after a lot of research and efforts. Why the heck did you spoil their fun by saying that?' we chided Amma at home.

But Amma being Amma, shot back immediately, 'Just because it's there in the Mahabharata, can we give a villainous name like "Duryodhana" to a child? One should choose a God's name that also sounds great. Other than being Virata Raja's wife, has Sudeshna accomplished anything great to deserve babies being named after her?'

Every morning, by the time we opened our main door, there would be a brown cow standing at the threshold. Amma would feed it daily with a little rice and jaggery from a brass basin. She'd also feed it cotton seeds, peeled fruit skins, lettuce and vegetable waste. It would leisurely eat everything and leave, only to return again the following day. If we happened to oversleep occasionally, it would make a loud noise by poking at the door latches with its horns and wake us up.

We didn't know who the owner of that cow was, but Amma loved it dearly. Once, when she was going to the Rayara Mutt, she spotted this cow chasing a scrawny stray cow. 'But the moment she saw me, you know how she stopped the chase and meekly stood aside with her eyes down? Trust me, these animals are way more loyal than us humans,' Amma said, after returning from the mutt.

However, it wasn't just the brown cow waiting for us every morning. Along with it, Rudramma, from the Old Well

Lane, would also wait. Rudramma wanted something very specific from the cow. Usually, right after eating the rice and jaggery Amma gave it, the cow would pass urine. Standing right behind the cow, Rudramma would eagerly wait for that moment. As soon as the cow started urinating, she'd cup both her hands and collect a palmful of cow urine, and gulp it down. Rudramma absolutely had no qualms while doing such a nauseous act. 'A thousand gods dwell in the body of a cow. Gomutra is the teertha of all those gods. If you drink two handfuls of this sacred water daily, you don't need to take any medicine all your life,' she'd declare if anyone asked her what she was doing.

Rudramma was so poor that she apparently dreaded having to buy expensive medicines more than anything else. Tired of seeing her drink plenty of gomutra every day, Amma once said, 'Wait a while longer, and the cow will take a dump too. Have a bellyful of cow dung too, and you can save spending on food as well.'

Angered by this, Rudramma went around town badmouthing Amma, declaring that 'the wretched woman is neither pious nor God-fearing'.

That didn't deter Amma from running down Rudramma. 'True, one has to respect the words of elders and mix a few drops of gomutra in the panchagavya and have it. But this woman sucks it as though it's gasa-gase payasa!' Amma would say.

This gomutra affair continued for several months. But one day, God knows what came over that cow—it forcefully kicked Rudramma, who was standing right behind it, her hands cupped and ready. The kick was so severe that poor Rudramma had to be hospitalized for over a fortnight, and had to swallow fistfuls of tablets day and night for months on end.

While we all felt very sorry for Rudramma, we felt equally angry with the cow as well. Severely thrashing it a couple of times, we also fiercely rebuked it face to face.

But Amma didn't approve of our ire towards the cow. 'I'm surprised why the cow hadn't kicked her until now. Come on, how do you like it if someone doesn't even let you pee in peace and waits to collect your urine by cupping their hands right behind you? Won't you go nuts? Tell me, yes or no. The poor thing has somehow put up with it for so long, only because she's a dumb creature,' Amma argued.

The way Amma equated the animals and humans in one sweep was bewildering. Even today, sometimes when I'm peeing, suddenly an image of someone trying to collect my urine in cupped hands comes to my mind, and I can't help but laugh.

There was a time when we used to strain coffee decoction by wringing it in a cloth. Later on, reasonably priced stainless steel filters came to the market.

Amma and I went to the steel utensils shop one day, bargained hard and brought home a new coffee filter. Amma put the coffee powder into the filter and poured in hot water to make the decoction. However, despite waiting for over two hours, not even a teaspoon of decoction seeped down. Although, one after the other, all of us at home smacked the coffee filter on its head multiple times, no decoction filtered down, and our desire to drink filter coffee couldn't be fulfilled. The next day, Amma and I went to the steel shop again.

'When can we drink coffee if it takes a month for a few drops of decoction to trickle down, Anna?' Amma complained, in her typical style of over-exaggerating.

The shopkeeper promptly started trying to fix the issue. As coffee filters were still rather newfangled, he also didn't know much about their functioning. Yet, he took out a steel poker and meticulously poked each hole in the strainer to make sure it worked. We took it back home, and poured coffee powder and hot water into it again. All of us were drooling with the hope of tasting filter coffee this time. But within a fraction of a minute, all the water dripped down with hardly any trace of coffee. We ran back to the steel shop again.

'Anna, all I asked you was to make the holes just big enough to let the decoction through, and you've made them so big that I could pass through them myself?' Amma demanded.

The ex-timid shopkeeper, who'd patiently dilated each and every hole of the strainer just the previous day, was of course, offended this time. He sized up Amma's tall and robust physique from head to toe for a minute.

He then placed the coffee filter before her and said, 'Go on, go through it. Let me see how you do it.'

For once, my otherwise witty Amma, who had a response for everything, was struck mute.

A Bellary girl once fell in love with a Malayali boy and they decided to get married. They met at work, and were so smitten that they wanted to get married. Meanwhile in Bellary, her parents had registered her name for the matrimonial services of the Madhwa Mandali and were eagerly scouting for a suitable groom by distributing photocopies of her horoscope to many suitors.

Just as they were anxiously waiting for a good alliance to come through, their daughter showed up with a curly-haired boy and introduced him as their son-in-law. When no amount of wailing and crying seemed to cut any ice with their only daughter, the parents somehow managed to console each other and grudgingly accepted their daughter's choice. Once the wedding date was fixed, they distributed invitation cards to all the relatives and friends. Wherever necessary, they said, 'Although the boy is Malayali, fortunately he's also a Brahmin only', and smiled sheepishly.

The wedding was to take place in the blistering month of April. A bus full of guests from the groom's side arrived from Kerala. None of them knew a word of Kannada. And our Bellary folks, of course, knew nothing other than Kannada and Telugu. But already, the bride had somehow learnt a bit of broken Malayalam. A handful of people could converse in English, though. As love is beyond language, in any case, the wedding proceedings were soon underway.

The blazing sun was taking a toll on everyone. Moreover, it was a three-day wedding, full of incomprehensible traditional rites and rituals. The guests from the groom's side were completely at sea and were trying their very best to cope with everything. The hosts earnestly tried to have animated conversations with the guests in Kannada. Although the guests didn't understand anything, with a wide smile on their face, they kept respectfully folding their hands for everything. Not understanding a single word of what the priest was uttering, the groom simply kept gaping at him like a dumbo. When the wedding band reached the crescendo, amid all the chaos, the bride instructed the groom to tie the thaali around her neck, and he did so. Finally, the wedding was over, and all the guests left.

Amma, of course, couldn't leave without executing her birthright of providing feedback about the wedding to the girl's parents. 'Such an amicable family! Especially your fellow in-laws, no grouse, no grumble. No matter what you said, for everything they'd simply stand with their hands folded, like the Hanuman on the brass handbell,' she quipped.

Not knowing how to fathom Amma comparing the groom's parents to Hanuman, they simply stood gawking at her.

Amma's sense of humour stayed intact even in her old age. Almost daily, after having their dinner, Amma–Appa would sit and chat with their medical kits spread out.

Once, with her nightly quota of tablets in hand, she asked me, 'Putta, they keep talking about drug addiction on TV, right? Actually, who is a drug addict? As you know, I also take so many drugs daily. Does it make me a drug addict?'

Although I was annoyed at her for disturbing my reading with such a silly question, I reassured her, saying, 'No, Amma, taking medicines in old age is not drug addiction.'

Stripping Appa's tablets out of their packaging, she'd pass them over to him and say, 'Let's see who'll be the first to check out of this world; will it be you or me?'

As reading became difficult with age, Amma gradually switched to watching more and more TV. As someone who'd been schooled in Bellary, she was drawn more to Telugu programmes than Kannada shows. She got hooked to a particular mega serial. It used to be aired exactly when Appa enjoyed his siesta.

Amma would not let Appa sleep and continuously asked him to watch the series with her. As Appa wasn't very adept in Telugu, Amma would translate most parts into Kannada for him. Slowly, Appa also developed a liking for the programme. Luckily, I used to be in the office during that serial time. But at night, while having dinner, Amma would take it upon herself to give me a blow by blow account of what was happening in the show. The popular series continued for over four years. Finally, one fine day, the marathon ended. A week later, Appa passed away.

After all the final rites and rituals were completed in Hampi, Amma, Akka and I were sitting in the front yard of our house and having a chat.

Speaking about Appa, Amma suddenly said, 'You know what? At the end of the day, your father's death is indeed a sacred one. Only because of his strong will could he hang on till the serial was complete.'

Unable to control our laughter, Akka and I guffawed loudly.

'While I'm sharing a serious matter with you guys, how can you laugh so thoughtlessly?' Amma grimly objected.

Amma wanted me to do the godaan within a year of Appa's death. Those days, I was living in England and wasn't sure I would find a cow to donate there. Amma kept asking me to make a quick trip home and be done with the godaan at the earliest. As I was busy with a very important project at that time, getting leave to come home was impossible.

'Your father will be stuck at the banks of the river Vaitarani,' she told me ominously. 'Vaitarani flows with all the filth, like blood, pus, urine, faecal matter and so on. Appa won't be able to cross it without a cow. In fact, he'd be waiting for you to perform the godaan in order to move ahead. He can't be stranded midway, you see.'

'But, Amma, even here we have the Thames River. There's a Venkataramana Swamy Temple on its banks. I'll take a holy dip right here in the Thames and give away the cow to the temple priest,' I reasoned.

Amma was horrified to hear that. 'Oh my God! England is the land of the mlecchas. There's no saying what barbaric practices people follow there. What if the priest slaughters and swallows the cow you give in charity? You must do the godaan here only.'

Amused by Amma's crazy views about England, I laughed to myself.

I couldn't do the godaan while Amma was still alive. She passed away when I was in England. To fulfil Amma's wishes, I went to Svadi, a pilgrimage in Karnataka, with Akka and her family. When we were there, Akka suggested that I do an exclusive godaan in Amma's name as well. But I thought that the cost of the godaan was rather high.

With the idea of saving some money, I cleverly asked the priest, 'Revered acharya, can I not make just one godaan for both my parents? Appa–Amma can ride on a single cow like Shiva–Parvathi and cross the Vaitarani together.'

Akka angrily chided me, saying, 'Will you stop using your engineering head at least here?'

But the priest didn't lose his cool and calmly said, 'Sorry, sir, actually Shiva and Parvati don't ride a cow, as their vehicle is a bull. Unlike the bull, a cow cannot bear the weight of two people. You'll have to do two independent godaans for each of your parents.'

In the face of his logic, I had no option but to say yes to two separate godaans.

Our ancestral home in my hometown had just one toilet. Like in most houses from those days, it was tucked away in the backyard. As Amma had become very weak due to old age, I thought of adding one more toilet attached to the house itself. Those days, Akka and her family used to stay with Amma in our house. As Akka went to work, it was Amma who mostly supervised the toilet construction work. Ironically, exactly two days after the toilet was ready to use, Amma succumbed to a massive heart attack right in that new toilet.

After all the final rituals were over, one day Amma's best friend and sometimes competitor, Gowramma, came to meet me to pay her condolences. Remembering Amma, she grieved incessantly, wondering how she'd be able to cope without her best friend. After crying substantially, she somehow managed to calm herself down in some time. She then wiped her tears and grimly said, 'Say what you will, but your Amma was indeed a tough lady. She just didn't let go of all the sweat she'd shed to have the new toilet built go in vain. She not only inaugurated it but also used it multiple times before meeting her maker. I'm glad she enjoyed the fruits of her labour in good time.'

Gowramma had spoken about Amma as though she was Kittur Rani Chennamma, who'd sacrificed her life for a noble cause! I could see Amma personified in the form of her friend Gowramma.

17

MOTHER IS NO GOD

7 May 2012

AMMA WAS AN EXPERT IN MAKING VERMICELLI kheer. She'd first prepare the dough with the right consistency and manually twist them into fine strands of shavige using her deft hands. She'd then put a small porcelain chip into fresh milk to prevent it from overflowing, and would start boiling it on a low flame. As the milk boiled, she'd keep stirring it with a steel ladle until she was satisfied by the texture.

I would curiously watch the process as the steel ladle touched the porcelain chip, creating a rhythmic hum, with every stir. Once the milk was ready, in a specific sequence, she'd mix the shavige, raisins and cashews—all fried separately in homemade ghee. She'd then add a little cardamom and saffron for flavour. Finally, when she'd add the sugar and stir the kheer, the aroma of the elixir would pervade the entire house.

Showing no restraint, Akka and I would gulp down tumbler after tumbler of kheer. Strangely, the payasam tasted even better the following day—so we'd always make sure we had enough to drink the next morning too. However, as Amma was diagnosed with diabetes rather early, she wouldn't drink any of the payasam herself.

But once, to everybody's surprise, even the nightingale sang out of tune! Yes, our ace chef once failed to deliver her signature payasa on a key occasion. Bragging about the glory of Amma's shavige payasa, we had invited some important guests home for lunch.

Nobody knew what was going on inside Amma's head that day. Quite unwittingly, she poured the tempering meant for lemon rice into the cauldron of payasa! Although she quickly realized her mistake and immediately scooped it out with a ladle, a part of the oggarane still got diffused in the boiling milk, and the milk turned the yellowish shade of the turmeric powder. Not much could be done to salvage the delicacy. As milk wasn't available round the clock in those days, preparing fresh kheer was out of the question. As there were no sweets shops in our town, a last-minute replacement for the payasa was also not possible. Moreover, our conscience didn't let us throw the expensive payasa into the gutter.

We complained bitterly and scowled furiously as we finished the payasa. Even the guests consumed the payasa with blatant grimaces. Appa, Akka and I relentlessly criticized Amma after the guests had left.

When we continued to grumble about it even while going to bed, Amma lost it totally. 'Do you guys think that I'm infallible, or what? Am I not entitled to a bad day like everybody else? I'm also a human being just like any of you. I'm no God, mind you,' she yelled furiously.

Listening to Amma's outburst, we shivered like sparrows drenched in the rain. Appa really had a tough time pacifying Amma that night.

The angry words Amma uttered that day still linger in my ears. Over time, those words have assumed new dimensions in my mind.

In India, we have a tendency to over-glorify a mother's love and her sacrifices. Through art and literature we place her on a pedestal and divinize her. In fact, I get irked to hear that clichéd term 'Thaayiye Devaru', which means a mother herself is God. One gets to hear it everywhere. When we ascribe divinity to mothers, we also presume that they have to be infallible. By doing this, we also portray her as an epitome of forgiveness. It makes it seem like it is her duty to forgive the faults and flaws of her husband and children. However, we refuse to make allowances for the mistakes and shortcomings of this God herself! We criticize her mistakes relentlessly. We exploit mothers with fallacies like 'to err is human and to forgive is divine'. When mothers toil all their lives and put other people first, we conveniently look away and take them for granted. We think that this is what is expected of them. But after they pass away, we flaunt king-sized photos of them in our living rooms and decorate it with fragrant garlands.

I often brood about the story of Parashurama, who is said to have massacred the entire community of Kshatriyas. He's the gentleman who, at his father's behest, barbarically beheaded his own mother merely because, in her youthful lust, she was briefly distracted by the sight of a king making love to his wife. I doubt if Parashurama would have been as cruel to his father, Jamadagni, if he had strayed and betrayed Renuka Devi!

Even today, I come across many children who have cut off all contact with their own mothers merely because they are unable to accept that their mother is as human as they are. There is no dearth of movies that depict kids of iniquitous women growing up as misogynistic characters and psychopaths.

A Goddess may be revered and worshipped, but she won't be loved and cared for. That's why there's a dire need to dethrone mothers from the pedestal of God and treat them as humans. We can shower our love and affection on her only when we look at her as a fellow human being. When she ceases to be a Goddess, it'll be easier for us to understand and accept her flaws and limitations.

Moreover, by divinizing the mother, we force her to accept the divinity being thrust upon her. It forces her to take responsibility for the mistakes of everyone else around her and makes her feel guilty for everything—even things she has absolutely no control over. She'll spend her entire life trying to please others. Quite unknowingly, she'll get exploited by everyone.

Amma's furious rebuttal is important to me in this context. Whenever Amma felt injustice was being meted out to her, she'd fight back. She had no qualms about going to the films with her friends, leaving Appa (who frowned upon films) behind. Nor was she sheepish about asking money from Appa in order to go watch these films. Whenever she went to Bellary or Hospet, regardless of Appa's resistance, she'd never board the bus without eating a masala dosa at a hotel. When I was working abroad, she sternly opposed to me living there, saying, 'If you go and settle down in some goddamn country, who'll take care of us? You better find yourself a job here and come back.'

Perhaps that's why Amma was never exploited by anyone. She demanded her fair share from me, Appa and

Akka, and got it. At the same time, she was generous with her love and affection. To others, she may have come off as haughty, but I genuinely regard her conduct as a mother to be an ideal one.

18

THE SERPENT OF ROPE

29 April 2012

OUR FAMILY USED TO OBSERVE OUR ELDERS' memorial days three times a year—the death anniversaries of both Ajja and Ajji, and the amavasye of Pitru Paksha. Appa–Amma used to conduct the rituals associated with these three holy days with a lot of devotion and faith.

For Ajja and Ajji's death anniversaries, Amma would prepare all the dishes that my grandparents enjoyed. Both Ajja and Ajji passed away before I was born. I hardly knew anything about them. However, on their death anniversaries, Amma used to describe their traits and qualities in great detail to Akka and me. From what I gathered, Ajja, although quite haughty and pompous otherwise, had very little tolerance for even minor pains. Feeling even slightly feverish was enough for him to get hyper panicky and create havoc and start throwing a fit. Once, when he was bitten by a scorpion, unable to put up with the fuss he was making, the family had apparently got a customized swinging cradle made for him in which they'd swing him to sleep—or, at least, this was what Amma told us. According to her, Ajja had a premonition of his death two days in advance. But strangely, he apparently surprised everyone by calmly accepting it as a fact of life! Consoling his grieving family members, he had allegedly asked his sons and daughters-in-law not to mourn his death, as it would amount to insulting Yamaraj himself.

Amma used to say that Ajji was a pious woman who loved her husband dearly. If she had to travel for any function, she would apparently chivvy her daughters-in-law to take good care of her husband. But about a year prior to Ajja's death, Ajji is said to have suffered total memory loss. 'She'd almost become like a child, you know? After that, she stopped keeping tabs on Ajja's breakfast, lunch and dinner every day as she earlier used to. Moreover, barely within half an hour of finishing her lunch, she'd ask me to serve it again. What followed was even worse ...' Amma would pause to sigh here. 'After the memory loss, her appetite increased abnormally. On the day of Ajja's death, looking at his body, she innocently asked me who was lying there in the living room. When I informed her about Mava's death, she paused and pondered over it for a minute, and then asked for some snacks to munch on, saying she was very hungry. Can you believe it?'

Appa was very impressed by the way Amma took care of his parents in their old age. 'Your mother would make such a good nurse, you know? Without ever detesting anything, she takes very good care of the bedridden,' Appa would say, time and again.

Archaka of the Rayara Mutt, Gundannacharya, was the priest who performed all the auspicious and inauspicious functions for all the Brahmin households in our town. Worthy of his name, Gundannacharya was indeed a very large man who took up much space. When he sat down on the floor, he occupied four large kadapa slabs. He had a remarkable appetite. He'd easily gobble up five holiges and ten vadas. He was very fond of ambode. People who marvelled at the sight of Gundannacharya eating countless ambodes lovingly gave him another alias—Ambode Achar. He lived up to it so well that over time people forgot his original name, and everybody called him Ambode Achar only.

In the afternoon, there would generally be some function in someone's house for which Gundannacharya would be called, and he would be fed there. He would then nap for a couple of hours before having his coffee. In the evenings, he had the habit of loafing around the entire town. All along the way, he'd stop at the several groups of idlers lining the roads and have a chat with them on just about anything. Be it politics, cinema, sports or even pure gossip, sniffing a spot of snuff every now and then, he'd spiritedly take part in every discussion. After having a satisfying conversation with diverse groups in town, he'd return home, have a large glass of milk and call it a day. As the Archaka of the Rayara Mutt, he was allowed only one meal a day. Eating breakfast and dinner was forbidden for Ambode Achar.

Gundannacharya had a large family of six daughters and three sons. His wife, Ragamma, often wept, remembering the three other kids she'd lost as infants. Obviously, it was hard for Achar to take care of his large family on his meagre income. But he didn't bother much about it.

In fact, if Achar's family somehow managed to make ends meet, it was thanks to Ragamma's smartness and austerity.

She'd cordially talk to everyone with love and affection, and provide solutions to their little hitches in religious practices. She treated everyone alike, regardless of the dakshine they paid. She always kept everyone in good humour. Not only Brahmins but even people of other castes loved and respected Ragamma. Every Thursday, through her children, she'd send panchamruta prasada in little cups to every house. After Rayara Aradhane, she'd make sure that everyone who'd paid for the seva received the prasadam.

Ragamma's general disposition inspired a lot of respect. Draping a nine-yard cotton saree like a dhoti; applying brown kumkuma vertically on her forehead; smearing a thick coat of turmeric on either cheek; adorning herself with a toe ring, anklets, a pearl nose pin, gold earrings and a dozen green glass bangles on both arms; and tying up her hair into a bun and decorating it with jasmine flowers, Ragamma had the presence of a true muttaide with a golden heart.

She'd shower love on all children. When people gave her Bagina, they'd put all its contents into a bag and send it with the children who went to escort her home. Struggling to match Ragamma's long strides, we'd be almost running behind her. She'd talk to us respectfully, like she talked to other elders. The only difference was that when she talked to children, she'd invariably add the suffix 'Devaroo', which means God, to almost every sentence: 'Be careful, Devroo,' 'Did you have your lunch, Devroo?' 'You should never miss your school, Devroo!' The list would go on. Once we'd reach her home, she'd ruffle our hair, caress our cheeks and ward off the evil eye by cracking her knuckles. We'd feel overwhelmed by her affection. She felt like a second mother to many of us.

At times, Ragamma would pour out her woes to Amma. 'Like a goat's tits, you guys cleverly stopped at just two kids. How could a poor village bumpkin like me know your smart urban ways, you tell me? In fact, I didn't even know the tricks of sleeping with my husband without getting pregnant. Whenever he called me to bed, without a word I meekly offered myself to him and went on delivering babies, like how pigs drop their litter. Now, while raising a battalion of kids, trust me, blood, not tears, trickle down my eyes,' she'd say, her voice choking with emotion.

I secretly enjoyed listening to the suggestive words , like 'tits', 'bed', 'pigs' and 'litter', in such conversations. Meanwhile, Ragamma's reference to the past glory of Amma's Bellary upbringing would make Amma swell like a balloon. But Amma had her coquettish ways of doing things. So, as if noticing me hanging around just then, she'd pinch my ears and say, 'You little rascal, look how you eavesdrop when adults are talking! Get out of here, you brat.'

Immediately, Ragamma would jump to my defence and say, 'Don't you scold my little Devroo like that. In fact, it's my mistake. I don't even have the common sense to discern when to say what and how.'

She'd then turn to me and say, 'You don't mind Amma's words, my Devroo. I'll give you a piece of jaggery, okay?'

Besides performing pooja for the Mutt and its devotees, all that Gundannacharya did was eat a sumptuous lunch in the afternoon and frivolously waffle on with folks in the evenings. He never bothered about any domestic responsibilities. Time and again, poor Ragamma begged him to go to the Mutt in the evenings and do an aarthi when the devotees visited, so that they could earn some extra dakshine.

But Gundannacharya just wouldn't forgo the joy of his idle evenings.

Eventually, Ragamma realized that she was fighting a losing battle and performed Upanayanam to her eldest son during the Aradhane so that he was eligible to offer aarthi to Rayaru. After the boy started going to the Mutt for the evening aarthi, they started seeing a few coins in the mangalaarthi tray. This helped Ragamma ensure all the children got porridge for breakfast daily.

Just as Ragamma's family was somehow keeping afloat, despite the challenges thrown their way by life, fate struck Gundannacharya in the form of diabetes. Once, when the Acharya had gone to perform a certain pooja in a doctor's house, as he was sprinkling the holy water, he suddenly fainted. The doctor got a blood test done and confirmed that his sugar levels were rather high. Apparently, diabetes had brought hypertension along as a companion. The doctor strictly advised him to totally stay away from sweets, fried and spicy snacks, and eat his food in moderation. Recommending lots of green vegetables and lettuce, the doctor also said that the Acharya shouldn't fast anymore. He was prescribed some tablets to take every day without fail for the rest of his life. The two rupees that came from the evening aarthi now had to be diverted towards the tablets.

The doctor apparently called the Acharya aside and told him in confidence that henceforth he shouldn't be fasting even on the days like Ekadashi and suggested that 'if not publicly, at least secretly you have to keep eating something or other every now and then. If possible, start having a few raw onions and raw garlic daily. It's really good for both diabetes and hypertension'. Instead of taking the doctor seriously, Gundannacharya went around openly disparaging the doctor, saying that 'the doctor has gone bonkers'.

Ragamma had never dreamt that such a trifle could spiral into wild twists. Gundannacharya's diabetes eventually ended up blowing out of proportion. For the first couple of months, he wore his diabetes diagnosis proudly, as though it was an accolade he'd painstakingly won, and pretended to stick to the strict diet. But the bloke had indulged in rich food for far too long to be able to suddenly change his ways. As old habits die hard, it wouldn't be fair to blame poor Gundannacharya for his vulnerability. Although Ragamma ensured that her husband didn't overeat at home, when he went to the devotees' houses to perform rituals, he'd more than make good for whatever he was deprived of at home. As everyone naturally fed a holy Brahmin generously, this became a big problem for Ragamma.

Whenever someone invited Gundannacharya for a memorial day function, Ragamma would go to their house in advance and profusely plead with them to be considerate. 'Please don't get me wrong, but I beg you not to feed my diabetic husband all the food that is made that day. Although he gobbles down everything with gluttony, his body just can't take it. So please serve him sparingly,' she'd implore.

But this seemed like a tricky situation to Amma. 'On the memorial day, the elders come home in the form of a Brahmin. If we don't satisfy them by serving whatever they want, won't we be cursed, Ragamma?' Amma asked.

'If you serve my husband all that he asks for, he'll soon check out of this world and you'll be guilty of the sin of widowing a Brahmin Muttaide, mind you.' Ragamma had hurled a deadly threat at Amma.

Since Amma didn't want the sin of killing off a Brahmin attached to her soul, she started serving the Acharya a little frugally. Evidently, it irked Gundannacharya, and he started grumbling about it openly. While on the one hand Amma feared Ragamma's wrath, on the other, she had to face the Acharya's ire. Clearly, Amma was caught between a rock and a hard place.

She shared her predicament with Appa.

'Now don't drag me into your women squabbles,' said Appa, trying to avoid the issue.

'Typical male escapism,' snapped Amma.

Eventually, Amma found a way out of the fix herself. The next time, she went to Ragamma's house and extended a joint invitation, saying, 'Both of you come home for the function as a couple.' So, on the memorial day, by lunchtime, Ragamma arrived with a copper pot and plate.

After that, Amma didn't have to take any decisions about the Acharya's diet herself. Before serving anything, she'd ask, 'Can I serve this, Ragamma?'

Ragamma would consider the item carefully and then say 'Just a little'; 'No, no rave-unde for him'; 'Just one small bit of ambode; actually, it's not allowed, but as it's his favourite, we have to make some allowances, you see …'

While Ragamma closely monitored her husband's intake, she had no hesitation in asking for a second and third helping of every dish for herself. Amma was relieved that whatever grouse Gundannacharya could now have would only be with Ragamma and not with her. However, sometimes Amma would get a little carried away and go a little overboard.

Once, even before serving rice for the main course, she asked Ragamma, 'Can I serve this?'

Gundannacharya got enraged by that and yelled, 'If you seek her permission to serve me rice the very first time itself, what do I eat, Amma? Do you want me to starve and die, or what?'

Gundannacharya secretly nursed a grudge against Amma for going behind his back and inviting Ragamma to oversee his diet. He waited for the right opportunity to take his revenge.

Once, fed up with the mounting family problems, Ragamma went to Mantralayam to perform Urulu Seve to Rayaru. After offering the service to Raghavendra Swami, she had directly gone to Bharamasagara to stay at her maternal home for about a fortnight. In the meantime, Ajja's memorial day had to be observed.

As usual, Amma went to Ragamma's house in advance and invited the Acharya for the annual ceremony. Although he had consented to come at that time, on the eve of the function, he came home and asked Amma to look for some other Brahmin, as he'd forgotten that he had committed to performing a Satyanarayana pooja that day.

When Amma piteously pleaded with the Acharya, he sternly declined, saying, 'You better look for someone who'll obediently have lunch as per his wife's wishes, Amma. Why do you want to have anything to do with a person like me?'

Ragamma wasn't in town to meditate on the matter. Without any other go, Appa–Amma had to travel to faraway Hospet to perform the ceremony at the Rayara Mutt there. When they returned home by dusk, Amma gave us a piece of rave unde as Ajja's prasadam. The bus fare and all the other expenses put together meant that my parents had spent two times the amount they usually did on the memorial service. That night, I saw Amma sitting in a corner and weeping softly.

After returning from Bharamasagara, Ragamma came running to our house. 'Sorry, Amma, my husband has not been fair to you at all. Indeed, he has made a big mistake. Please show some magnanimity and forgive us. You've trusted us for generations to perform all the good and bad rituals for your family. My husband has committed a blunder in my absence. Please forgive us this once, and I assure you that it will never happen again.'

But the Acharya had tasted success and enjoyed keeping Amma on tenterhooks. Whenever Amma tried to pre-book his services for an upcoming annual ceremony, he'd say, 'Actually, I have some other commitments on that day. You do one thing. You just go to Hospet like you did last time.'

Although he was simply unleashing a serpent of rope to scare Amma, these false alarms would keep her on edge until the ceremony was over. Amma would go and plead with Ragamma to intervene and fix the issue. Eventually, Amma realized the crux of her mistake and stopped inviting Ragamma along with the Acharya.

Though this strategy provided some respite to Amma, she was still upset with the Acharya for unleashing serpents of rope to keep her on tenterhooks. Although she didn't show it overtly, she was secretly waiting to get even with the Acharya.

And that day did arrive.

A new priest, Balacharya, happened to move into our town. Earlier, he used to live in a village near Kudligi, earning his livelihood from performing puja at a Rayara Mutt there.

It was a small village with about twenty Smartha and ten Madhwa households. Although there was no significant income in terms of dakshine, the temple had two acres of land in its name. Balacharya had leased out the land to a local farmer in exchange for the millets and vegetables required for his family to survive. But two major developments took place in the village prompting Balacharya to migrate.

The Smartha Brahmins, who outnumbered the Madhwa Brahmin population in the village, got together and built a Shankara Mutt for themselves, and installed a Shivalinga as well as an idol of Goddess Sharada Devi. After that, the Smarthas stopped visiting Rayara Mutt frequently. Balacharya could have still sustained that blow. But with the tiller of the land getting the ownership after the implementation of the Land Reforms Act, the farmer who was tilling the mutt's land claimed its ownership and got it. Although some Brahmins tried to dissuade the farmer with threats like, 'Don't take the risk of usurping Guruvarya's land and inviting God's wrath', and 'You'll face dire consequences if you take over Mutt's property', the farmer defiantly countered, saying: 'You're always cribbing about your hardships only. Come to my house once and try to know about my difficulties as well. Let's talk about the Guruvarya afterwards.'

As the law was on the farmer's side, Balacharya and his family came to the streets. Citing the plight of Balacharya's family, a few leaders of the village sent an appeal to the seer at Mantralayam. But no one seemed interested in rescuing a temple without much income.

One day, Balacharya offered a special pooja and extensive oblations to Rayaru, prostrated before him, and said, 'Oh, Raghappa, apparently I am not destined to make a living here anymore. I'm calling it quits here to move on in search of my livelihood. Kindly guide me in the path ahead.' Having taken the blessings of his beloved deity, with bag and baggage, and a heavy heart, Balacharya landed in our town—which town was relatively bigger and had quite a few Brahmin families.

Balacharya was an intelligent man. As he was highly proficient in Sanskrit, he chanted hymns with impeccable diction. People who listened to his scholarly sermons were floored by his oratory skills. Gradually, his popularity soared. Amma realized that the day she had been waiting for had finally come.

Although there were only two days left for Ajji's memorial, she hadn't invited Gundannacharya yet. However, the Acharya was well aware of the memorial day schedule of every family in town. After waiting as long as he could, he asked Amma up front, 'What time do you want me to come for the ceremony the day after tomorrow?'

Daintily positioning her nose pin, Amma unleashed a serpent of rope, saying, 'This time we've invited Balacharya.'

Gundannacharya got scared. The income from annual memorial ceremonies was crucial for him to run his family. 'Oh, come on, Amma, how can you do this to me?' Acharya asked, laughing sheepishly.

'Acharre, I know you've a very large clientele and have little time for people like us these days. But we can't really stop doing ceremonies because you are too busy, can we?' asked Amma, adding insult to injury.

By evening, Ragamma came home and pleaded, 'Please have mercy on us, Amma. If loyal clients like you start deserting us like this, we'll have to starve to death.'

'Oh, come on, Ragamma. Don't you know that we'll never betray you? It's just that I'm sick of the fake snake threats your husband keeps throwing at me. Don't you worry, just let him have a taste of his own medicine for a while,' Amma reassured her and gave her a cup of coffee.

Lately, Ragamma had been feeling very insecure about her husband's profession. 'I heard that Balacharya is a highly knowledgeable Sanskrit scholar. Everyone is so impressed with his diction of the hymns. And my man, as you know, is a dork. Instead of giving spiritual sermons in the evenings, he loves to idly chat with wastrels. At this rate, I don't know what will happen to us,' said Ragamma, sharing her fears.

Comforting Ragamma, Amma gently pressed her hand and said, 'Ayyo, don't you worry, Ragamma. I'm quite well versed with the ways of our folks. We make a big deal out of trivia. How does it matter if one's chanting of the hymns is great or otherwise? No one understands it anyway. All that matters is whether one is uttering some gibberish while doing the pooja or not. Worry not. Yours is a family that's been in priesthood for generations. No one will ditch you for such silly reasons.'

Listening to Amma, Ragamma felt a lot better. However, Amma didn't stop letting out rope serpents on Acharya.

Days passed by. As age mellowed people down, they lost interest in setting traps for others to fall into. After I found a job in Bangalore, Appa and Amma moved in with me. We lost touch with Ragamma soon. Although initially Appa–Amma kept visiting our hometown once in a while, even that became rare after Appa's health deteriorated.

As Appa used to say, there was indeed a compassionate caregiver in Amma. She took very good care of Appa. When his right arm lost strength, she'd affectionately feed him with her own hands and drape him in the dhoti, as though he was a toddler. When his digestion gave way, she started making porridge for him. Despite all her care, Appa suddenly passed away one fateful night.

As per Amma's wishes, we took Appa to our town for cremation. Ragamma had come home to pay her condolences. 'Despite doing all the poojas and vratas, why didn't God bless me with Muttaide's death, Ragamma?' Amma cried to her.

Patting Amma's shoulders, Ragamma said, 'These things are not in our hands, you see. In the lure of a young wife, these men end up marrying girls much younger than them. When that's the case, how can we expect to die before they do, you tell me? If one still wants Muttaide's death, maybe one has to consume poison, I guess.'

Overhearing Ragamma, a couple of other women who had come home to meet Amma sniggered. For once, Amma didn't have a response and simply gawked at Ragamma.

In about a year, Amma also passed away. Again Ragamma came to our house and soothed me with her comforting words. 'Never ever consider yourself as a motherless orphan, my child. Remember, from today, I am a mother of ten and not nine,' she said, caressing my face.

After Appa–Amma passed away, I almost stopped visiting our town. I eventually went home only to sell our house. While I was there, I heard that 'Ambode Acharya' had died about a year ago and went to visit Ragamma. It was heart-wrenching to see her leading the life of an ordained widow—with her tonsured head and red saree.

'What's this, Ragamma? Why did you do this? I just can't bear to see you like this,' I said, teary-eyed.

'What could I do, Devroo? The Almighty cursed me with widowhood,' she said, letting out a heavy sigh.

'It's true that we all have little choice but to endure God's will. But what was the need to inflict such a terrible avatar on yourself? Did Amma shave her head like this? Times have changed, Ragamma; it's time we put an end to these heinous practices,' I said irritably.

'My matter is a little sensitive, Devroo. All these years, we have earned our livelihood in the name of traditional dharmic rites and rituals. What will people say if we abandon all these practices at a time like this? Your father, on the other hand, was a government employee. Naturally your mother didn't have the constraints that I do. My case is totally different, Devroo,' she reasoned.

Before taking leave, I prostrated myself in front of her.

'In spite of being in a respectable job, you have come all the way to meet this old woman. Few people have such humility these days. May God bless you, Devroo,' she said, blessing me.

I never got an opportunity to meet her again. Two years ago, I heard that she passed away. Her children apparently are doing various odd jobs at different places. Someone else is running the Rayara Mutt.

All the Brahmin families that I saw in my childhood were very poor. So much so that having two meals a day used to be a luxury for them. Most of them couldn't afford to buy a pair of new clothes for their children even once a year. The credit of them somehow scraping by goes to smart women like Ragamma. Without their support and blessings, our generation could not have acquired the kind of upbringing and education that we did. We should be thankful to them for having enabled us to build reasonably secure and lucrative careers for ourselves.

Now most of us are no longer interested in their beliefs and practices. By and large, we have accepted a modern lifestyle. At the same time, it's also true that I rarely get to see pure souls like Ragamma in these modern times. Maybe my age is also one of the reasons for that.

19

CHUKKI BALEHANNU

2 April 2016

'CHUKKI BALEHANNU' LITERALLY TRANSLATES TO 'dotted bananas'. What this means is that they are regular Robusta bananas that are a little overripe, so they have black dots on their peel. In Kannada, we colloquially call them 'chukki balehannu'. In Bellary's heat, bananas tend to get ripe faster than in other places. However, these bananas were not readily available in our town. We had to get them from either Hospet or Bellary city, and they would usually come to the markets only in the evenings.

My family loved these bananas. Whenever Appa or Amma went to Bellary, they'd invariably bring home a dozen or two with them. This apparently simple task of bringing bananas home wasn't easy, though. Only a couple of government buses plied to our town in the night. No private buses operated on these routes. One had to catch either the Mantralayam–Kudligi bus or the Koppal–Bangalore one. As both were long-distance buses, passengers with reservations or those travelling from end to end were given priority. As our town was barely 50 kilometres away, one could not expect a seat on these buses. Moreover, since Bellary was the district headquarters, any bus from there would be jam-packed. To safeguard a dozen bananas from getting mangled in such overcrowded buses was nothing less than Mission Impossible. Despite taking utmost care, if a couple of bananas still got crushed, Amma would feed them to the monkeys in the neem tree in our backyard. Almost everyone who went to Bellary from our town would return with a huge bunch of bananas in hand.

More often than not, buses would get late in reaching our town. However, no one blamed the poor drivers who patiently manoeuvred their old clunkers through our pothole-ridden, bumpy roads and still managed to reach all the destinations along the way, albeit a little late. At home, Akka and I would stay awake and wait as long as we could—in anticipation of the bananas coming home, if not other, more interesting snacks. But despite our best efforts, we'd often slip into our dreams.

As we had instructed them to wake us up no matter when they arrive, Appa–Amma would rouse us, saying, 'Come on, kiddos, get up. We have brought dotted bananas for you guys.'

On hearing the words 'dotted bananas', we'd immediately sit up with our hands stretched out. Our bellies always had the space for just another dotted banana. We'd hurriedly swallow a few and quickly return to sleep.

Amma would often say that the gods simply loved chukki balehannu. So every time we brought some home, Amma would take a few either to the Rayara Mutt or the Hanuman temple at the town's entrance to offer to the gods. Of course, our neighbours too would expect a couple of bananas. The tonsured widow, Kashavva, who used to live in the ell of our house, would assertively demand her share in the portion of bananas brought home. 'This time, give me three chukki balehannu, Amma. One for the panchamruta and the other two, of course, for my night phalaara,' she'd say. Sometimes, she'd urge Appa to put in a word with Amma about being a little more generous while handing out bananas. Being a widow, Kashavva was allowed only one meal a day. Since she'd lost her husband at a very young age, she couldn't even remember having a proper dinner at night. Going to Bellary and buying these special bananas were beyond her means.

In our town, the belief was that if babies are excessively whiny, a smear of this special banana's pulp would instantly soothe them. So, it was not uncommon for new mothers to plead with Amma, or with their other neighbours, for a few such dotted bananas. If we had any bananas at home, Amma would readily give them away. Otherwise she'd suggest something like, 'Why don't you check with so-and-so? Apparently, she'd been to Bellary for some shopping just the other day.'

Even the skin of these dotted bananas held value. Everybody in town knew that the fibrous content in the banana skin had medicinal value in easing out constipation. Victims of constipation gouged out the fibrous inside of the banana skin and had it before sleeping. It was claimed that the next morning they would be absolutely fine and could use the bathroom in peace.

Quite obviously, constipation is rather common among people who live in the scorching heat of a water-scarce town, and yet thrive only on formidably hot and spicy food. In our town, at least one person in every household had to deal with the challenge of breaking the bottleneck every morning. This ensured that the slimy inner layers of the banana skin were in huge demand. Since we kids had no pooping problem, we frowned at the not so tasty banana skin.

Even the residual bare skin had some utility. People used all the shaved-off banana skin to distract houseflies by stocking it in enamel-coated brass bowls, which they'd keep at a distance in their backyards. Lured by the flavour of the dotted banana's skin, the houseflies would confine themselves to swarming around the brass bowls in the backyards and stayed away from the house.

Unlike many other households in our town, we didn't rear a cow. However, Amma had befriended a beautiful, brown-coloured cow with white patches. Every morning, the cow would come and stand by our main door, and wait for Amma to feed her jaggery rice and the leftovers from the previous day, along with all the vegetable waste. She would eat everything put before her. We would put a smear of kumkum on her head and feed her.

The cow loved dotted bananas very much. Whenever there were dotted bananas at home, the cow would somehow smell it, and get restive and fidgety. On such days, she wouldn't have the patience to wait until we opened the door on our own. Knocking on the door latches with her horns, she would keep mooing loudly as if there was no tomorrow. We, the kids, didn't have the courage to carry the feeding bin and place it before the cow on such occasions. While she was agitated, even the elders didn't dare to smear the kumkum on her forehead until she was satiated after eating the banana skin.

After she was pacified, Amma would circumambulate the cow, fondly smack her on the belly and chide her, saying, 'You gluttonous wretch.'

I could never find dotted bananas while I was in England. In every supermarket, they'd have either yellow-coloured or greenish-yellow bananas only. I didn't know an English term for our chukki balehannu. I wasn't sure if I'd be able to convey exactly what I wanted by literally translating it as 'dotted bananas'! In the cold weather of England, though overripe bananas turned black, they seldom developed dots.

However, once when I was buying groceries in a supermarket, in an obscure corner of a shelf I spotted four dotted bananas. My joy knew no bounds as I grabbed them and nearly ran towards the counter.

The moment the cashier noticed the bananas in my hands, she apologetically took them away from me and said, 'Extremely sorry, sir. They are spoilt already. I guess you didn't notice the black spots on them. Don't worry, I'll get you the fresh ones.'

I smiled at her and said, 'No, no, don't bother, please. They're perfect. In fact, just the stuff I needed.'

'No way. I can't sell these rotten fruits to you. I'm sorry,' she said decisively.

'Okay then, give them to me for free,' I insisted.

'Sorry sir, I can't take that risk. In case you eat these rotten fruits and something happens to you, it'll be our responsibility. It's not just about your health alone, I can't stake our store's reputation, you know!'

'But then, what will you do with these?' I asked, curiously.

'I'll throw them into a dustbin for now and will dispose of them later.'

Not knowing what to say, I silently walked out of the supermarket, leaving my precious bananas behind. Through the large glass window, I could see the salesgirl animatedly explaining something to the attendant and pointing to the bananas.

20

FIVE PAISE DOWRY

4 July 2015

I DON'T KNOW WHY THESE CHILDHOOD MEMORIES are lingering in my mind today. That year I'm remembering, two little kids had come to stay in our house for some time from a faraway town. They were distant relatives of Appa's. The older one, Pranesha, was about ten years old. His sister, Sudha, was about seven.

Pranesha and Sudha came from an indigent family of modest means. As they were of the same age as Akka and me, respectively, Appa had invited them over to our house so that the four of us could enjoy our vacation together.

Both Pranesha and Sudha were sharp and active. As soon as they came to know about the water scarcity in our town, they started accompanying us to the tap pit with brass pots to help us fetch water, saying, 'We are quite adept at carrying water, as we have the same problem in our town as well.'

Sudha used to sit with Amma and help her sort the lettuce. She was very well-behaved and never threw tantrums about missing her parents. Dressed in a red skirt and a yellow top, Sudha would move around the house, filling the air with her giggles and the jingle of her anklets. Pranesha, on the other hand, would drape his little angavastram as a dhoti, gaudily smear the Gopichandana on his forehead, and sit in the hallway and do Sandhyavandane.

It was the month of October, when our town is surrounded by greenery. Usually, it's when all the kids of our town team up to pay a customary annual visit to the Gandi Narasimha Swamy Temple, located about six kilometres from our town. Incidentally, as our maternal uncle, our Mava, was also visiting us around the same time, he assumed the responsibility of taking the whole battalion of kids to the temple.

We carried bisibele bath and curd rice packed from home. After praying at the temple, we played to our heart's content and then settled on the banks of a rivulet to eat. Digging little water springs alongside the rivulet, we quenched our thirst. After playing with the monkeys for some more time, we happily headed home.

Near our town's entrance, a new restaurant had come up. Mava took all of us to the new restaurant. We had never gone to a restaurant in our own town. Sometimes, when we went to Bellary or Hospet, Appa would occasionally treat us to a masala dosa. As Appa didn't approve of going to a local restaurant unnecessarily, we were a bit scared to enter. However, Mava instilled confidence in us and bought coffees for all of us. We all were thrilled to drink coffee in our town's restaurant for the first time.

As Amma had insisted that we return home before it got dark, we hurriedly left the restaurant and scurried towards home. We had barely taken a few steps when, 'Prananna… Pranannaa,' Sudha yelled, anxiously.

'What's up, Sudha puttee?' asked Pranesha.

'Er … the coffee was too hot … I couldn't really finish it fully. Actually, I could have only half of it, the other half I left in the tumbler only,' confessed Sudha.

Hearing that, Pranesha was visibly scared and said, 'We've had it if Amma gets to know of it.' He then ran back to the hotel in a flash.

Even before we could understand what was going on, Pranesha returned with a smile on his face and said, 'Don't worry, Sudha, I finished the leftover coffee, we don't need to fear any scolding now.'

Sudha seemed relieved to know that.

Now, when we think of such incidents, they seem funny. But in our childhood, we didn't dare waste any food for fear of being scolded by our parents. On top of it, by linking it to some religious beliefs, our elders ensured that we didn't throw away anything. For instance, everyone believed that Goddess Lakshmi would desert you if you left any food unconsumed on your dinner plate. Although all of us were poor already, we still feared that Lakshmi would leave us! Despite haunting poverty, everyone sincerely believed in such myths.

Occasionally, despite Amma's strict vigil over the vegetables she used in her cooking, a couple of bitter cucumbers or corns would somehow find their way into her curry or salad. But even on such days, Appa would finish his plate to a sparkle. He would clear his plate with such impeccable finesse that Amma eating from the same plate never seemed awkward to us.

On festival days, we'd obviously have quite an assorted menu. With so much food available, Akka and I would end up grabbing more food than we could finish. Appa didn't like to scold us for wasting food on a festival day but he couldn't bear to see the food being wasted either. However, he soon found a way to solve this problem.

'Whoever finishes all the food on their plantain leaf, leaving no trace behind, will get a reward of five paise,' he'd declare right at the beginning.

Those days, five paise was big money for us! We'd carefully ensure that Amma served only as much as we could eat and finished every dish and grain of rice on the leaves placed in front of us. So much so that, in the end, we'd even wipe off the small spot of salt served in one corner of the leaf.

After Amma removed all the plantain leaves and mopped the floor, Appa would confirm with her that Akka and I hadn't cheated—he wanted to make sure that we hadn't hidden any food under the leaf or anything. He'd then hand out the reward as promised. Feeling so proud of having earned a big sum, we'd start talking about the things we'd buy with that money. Amma would crib about Appa's generosity and chide him for spoiling young kids by giving them money.

If Appa had to ever cite an example, he would look no further than animals.

'Ever seen a wild animal being obese?' he'd ask. 'Obesity bothers only humans and pet animals. Once a tiger has had his meal, he wouldn't bother to even touch you, even though you are next to him, you know? Once its needs are satiated, it's no longer greedy like us. It's only us humans who store rice, wheat and pulses for the entire year. Indeed, the wild beasts are far wiser than us.'

The five paise reward that Appa used to give us still haunts me from time to time. Whenever I know that I am buying more than what I need, the thought of that five paise coin pops up in my head. Despite having enough clothes, when I'm tempted to buy new ones, an image of a five-paise coin appears before my mind's eye. While exchanging an old TV that's still working just fine for the latest model, I feel as if that five-paise coin is sneering at me. If I am rummaging through a drawer to find that misplaced stapler and I only find a host of things I've bought on a whim and have no use for, Appa's coin smirks at me with contempt.

I feel Appa's five-paise concept, if understood properly, has the potential to change the world. It certainly has the ability to rein in all my unnecessary hankerings.

Here is another story that I have suddenly remembered. It is a rather funny incident that involves my otherwise very austere Appa.

Amma wasn't particularly fond of house pets, like cats and dogs. In fact, traditional Madhwa households that meticulously follow all the rites and rituals can have little room for pets. But somehow, a sick mongrel found its way to our backyard and ended up staying there. Despite Amma driving it away repeatedly, it still returned to our backyard for some reason. Probably it yearned to gobble up the leftovers of Amma's delicious food. But waiting perpetually in the backyard of a household that never wasted even a speck of food, the poor dog was quite disappointed.

Noticing the dog getting more and more despondent every day, Appa felt bad. Quickly, he found a way to address the issue. As a conservative Madhwa, before every meal,

Appa did parishechana and offered chitrahuthi to the gods by setting aside a few grains of rice next to his plate. From that day onwards instead of a few grains, Appa started to keep a chitrahuthi of four sizeable morsels.

Initially, we didn't understand what he was doing. When probed, Appa evasively said, 'The Acharya has said that the gods bless good things upon the houses that keep a generous chitrahuthi.'

But in a couple of days, Amma found out the real reason behind it and cribbed, saying, 'All this drama is your Appa's ploy to somehow feed that bloody mongrel in the backyard.'

Even now, whenever I attend any function, I keenly observe people's eating habits. Whether it's a buffet or a regular meal served on plantain leaves, quite inadvertently my eyes tend to browse over the plates or leaves and take stock of the leftover food. It gives me a fair idea about the kind of crowd that has attended the function. For me, it's not just about India's poverty and hunger index. Although they are indeed serious concerns, I regard wasting food as an ethical issue. I wish everybody would rein in their greed for overconsumption and strive to get Appa's five paise.

'Why should we force ourselves to eat something that isn't tasty?' is an oft-heard argument. But I don't subscribe to that view. Let alone eating, many times, life itself forces us to accept things we don't really like. Then why make a fuss about food alone? The sky won't fall on our heads if we eat something tasteless occasionally. It's a way of honouring the hands that cook and serve us. Of course, I wouldn't insist that people should eat food even if it's tainted or rotten. But I just can't approve of wasting food merely because it isn't tasty enough.

Recently, my niece got married. As a mother, my sister was naturally worried about things like how her son-in-law and his family would turn out. In arranged marriages, where alliances come through the mediation of some remote acquaintances, little can be known about the character of the groom or his family. Although the parents of the boy and girl proceed with the alliance because the horoscopes match, they often get their first glimpse into the true nature of each other's families only on the day of the wedding.

In my niece's wedding, after all the formalities were done with and everybody finished their lunch, as usual, my roving eyes quickly scrutinized the leftover plantain leaves. The groom had cleared his plantain leaf, leaving nothing. Both his parents had also eaten cleanly, leaving no morsels behind.

I called Akka, showed her their leaves, and said, 'Rest assured, Akka, the groom is a good boy without any ego. Even his family seems to be quite cultured.'

Akka seemed relieved to hear that.

'Time to give the credit where it's due. Our son-in-law has rightfully earned his five-paise dowry, right?' I asked Akka.

Knowing what I was talking about, Akka heartily laughed with me.

21

EMPATHY: THE KEY TO WORLD PEACE

2 January 2015

THERE'S NOTHING SPECIAL ABOUT THE INCIDENT that took place in our house. Almost everyone staying in Bangalore for a few decades or more would have experienced it in one form or another. But that incident had a strong impact on me. I've brooded over it in multiple ways. Over the years, in different times and circumstances, I have marvelled at various truths it has unveiled before me. It has inspired me to understand myself, and others around me. Let me share some of those thoughts with you here.

It was the latter half of the 1990s. Both my parents had moved with me to Bangalore from our ancestral home in our native place. I had already completed about seven to eight years in the software industry by then. We were staying in a rented, independent house in BTM Layout. Although my salary was rising slowly, it wasn't very high yet. Around this time, I started considering buying a plot to build a house. But Amma wasn't very keen on the idea. 'When we already have a nice house in our town, why do you want to build another house here? After all, we'll have to eventually go back home and settle there only, right? No matter how long we stay here, this city can never become ours, can it?' she'd ask.

Interpreting the *Dasara Pada, Allide Nammane illiruvudu Summane*, in her own way, she firmly believed that our bonding with Bellary was eternal and regarded our stay in Bangalore as just transitory.

But the woman in the neighbouring house fed the idea of buying a plot of land into Amma's head. 'Ask your son to buy a site. It's not as if you must build a house there. If you just keep it for five years and sell it off, it'll easily fetch you tenfold. It's so much better than parking your money in fixed deposits,' she told Amma.

Tempted by the term 'profits', Amma softened her stance and asked me to even explore some options. Of late, Appa had stopped voicing his opinion on such important matters and silently approved all my decisions. Ever since had I landed my first job, Appa seemed to have lost the confidence to contradict his educated son, who earned way more than he ever did.

Buying something that has already been bought before seems like no big deal. But buying something big like a plot of land for the first time feels quite thrilling. Maybe because it's a high-value commodity, but we tend to get even more anxious while making such purchases. On the whole, for people with moderate means, making a decision like buying a plot of land suddenly opens up a Pandora's box of anxieties:

What exactly is its real value? Is anyone trying to take us for a ride? Is it really wise to invest such a huge amount of money in a plot of land in the first place? What if the property has some ongoing litigation?

Usually, people prefer to buy a plot of land or a house in the surroundings of their current residence. It's an interesting example of the natural human resistance to change. I was no different. I focused my search around the BTM Layout. In those days, BTM Layout was still a remote, deserted extension to the vibrant city of Bangalore. By eight at night, an eerie silence would prevail across its vacant streets. Few dared to step out after dusk. 'If someone knocks you down, not a soul will know until dawn,' Amma would say.

Some of my friends who were born and bred in Bangalore lived in prime areas like Jayanagar, Basavanagudi and Malleshwaram. 'BTM Layout is so far away. Why don't you look for a site somewhere nearby?' they'd suggest. But there were hardly any plots of land available in those prime localities. Even when I found a few vacant plots sporadically, they either cost a fortune or had some litigation ongoing in courts.

I contacted quite a few real estate agents. Typically, 'Do you believe in Vastu?' used to be their first question. I didn't know anything about Vastu. I'd never heard anyone talking about Vastu in my hometown. I discussed it with Amma.

Apparently, she'd heard a few things about Vastu. 'Look, we lived in puny little houses in some nook and corner of Bellary's narrow lanes and alleys. On a small piece of inherited land, we somehow managed to build a mud structure like a railway compartment and lived in it. Although our houses didn't have proper light and ventilation, we somehow managed to live our lives quite happily in those dingy abodes. So things like Vastu have never mattered to us. All that stuff is the fancy of the wealthy,' she declared.

Although I was employed and earned a decent living, Appa–Amma still considered themselves poor.

Meeting my agent, I said that I wasn't very particular about Vastu.

He couldn't hide his delight. 'In that case, I'll readily show you a hundred sites,' he declared.

Every evening and on weekends, he showed me plots upon plots of land. After showing each site, 'How do you like it, sir?' he'd ask.

I didn't know what to say. In fact, I had no idea what parameters rendered a plot good or bad. But I eventually liked one of the sites for some reason.

It was a plain 60×40 corner plot, away from the hubbub of traffic. The agent took me to its owner to strike a deal. The plot owner needed money badly. Finally, the deal came through for eight lakh rupees. I took Appa–Amma and showed them the plot. They liked it as well. I paid the advance and locked the deal.

But there was a hitch that only I knew about. My total savings at the time wasn't more than four lakh rupees, and my salary was also quite modest. But one of my friends had told me that I could avail a loan to purchase the plot. Those days, though, most banks lent money to build or purchase houses; they didn't offer credit to buy plots of land. When I enquired with a private bank, considering my company credentials and monthly salary, they assured me that they would grant me the loan. That's how I was all set to go ahead with my plans.

However, I had not informed Appa–Amma about taking a loan yet.

One afternoon, about a week before the proposed registration of the plot, as we were having lunch at home, I casually mentioned that I was taking out a loan to buy the land. The moment I said so, 'Are you taking on a debt?' Amma asked in disbelief.

I nodded my head nonchalantly. Crestfallen, she started crying at once.

Just as I was wondering how to pacify her, she suddenly vowed loudly, 'No matter what, as long as I am alive, I won't let my son become a debtor.'

I was shocked by the intensity with which she said that. Although I tried to explain how these things worked, she was not in a state to listen to me. As Appa didn't want to get involved in such matters, he stayed quiet. Sensing that Amma was too worked up, I thought I'd defer the matter for the time being.

However, even after several days, Amma firmly stood her ground! She just couldn't stomach the idea of her son owing a debt. Being the stubborn woman that she was, she'd do whatever it took to have her way. As I knew that it was impossible to persuade her to change her mind, I dropped the idea of buying the plot altogether. I had to let go of the advance I'd already paid.

Although I took it in my stride, I was hurt when the plot owner sarcastically taunted me, saying, 'Why did you have to proceed this far when it was a deal beyond your means?'

The agent who was upset about losing his commission asked, 'How will you survive in this big city if you keep listening to such old village chumps?'

I decided to stay away from all real estate agents for the time being and vowed not to think about buying a plot of land until I had the eight lakh rupees in hard cash.

By the time I accumulated that amount, the price of land in BTM Layout had crossed eighteen lakh rupees. I cursed myself for being stupid enough to fall for Amma's foolish principles. Anger started building up inside me. Whenever Amma tried to participate in any decision-making, I'd very rudely snub her, saying, 'You just shut up.' If we happened to pass that plot of land I was going to buy, I'd show her the mansion that had come up there and chide her, 'See! If only you hadn't come in the way, that mansion out there would be ours today.'

Fed up with my taunts, one day she folded her hands in mock reverence and said, 'Forgive me, my lord. I was too naive then and didn't know better. But rest assured, I won't interfere in any of your affairs henceforth.'

Her bitter words made me realize my cruelty, and I stopped raising that matter before her after that.

Somehow, I could never buy a plot of land while my parents were still alive. Both Appa and Amma passed away within a span of one year. Later, I bought a flat in an apartment complex and moved in there. Nowadays, I've lost interest in material things like land and houses. These days, when I pass that plot of land I had intended to buy, the memories come rushing back, but without the bitterness and regret I'd let fester inside me for a long time.

As I said earlier, this incident has inspired many thoughts. I regret how much I fought with Amma for not letting me take a loan. She'd developed her beliefs based on her own experiences, and her experiences had taught her that taking out loans was bad. That's why she didn't want her son to get into debt and opposed it strongly. Those days, I didn't have the maturity to understand her perspective. In a world where availing credit is regarded as a path to progress, I couldn't appreciate her age-old principles.

I'm reminded of an incident from my childhood. I had a maternal uncle. Mava was Amma's only brother. He was quite well-to-do. Whenever Appa–Amma ran short of money, they'd borrow some cash from Mava and would return it as soon as they could. He was very fond of Amma, and never hesitated to help her in tough times. But on one occasion Mava himself got into some financial problems and asked Amma for a loan.

With Appa's meagre income, we often struggled to make ends meet towards the end of the month. So, Appa–Amma were in no position to lend money to him. However, Mava had always stood by them whenever they needed money, and they couldn't let him down now. Finally, they found a way out. Amma pledged some of her gold jewellery in the bank and raised a loan against it. Appa sent that money to Mava, along with a request to return it as early as possible. Mava was indeed very grateful for the timely help.

Appa–Amma suffered greatly till they brought back the gold they had pledged. Every month, they had to pay a big amount as interest to the bank. It was a big burden on our already shoestring budget. Due to this additional outflow, month ends became even more challenging. We didn't get any new clothes for Ugadi that year. Amma didn't prepare the usual festival delicacies. The lamps in the pooja room no longer remained lit round the clock. Unable to sleep, Appa–Amma kept rolling in bed all night.

Although we were too young to understand the intense ordeal our parents were going through at that time, I clearly remember us being really anxious seeing them suffer like that. Now, when I look back, all their suffering and anxiety seem distant, from an era bygone. Frugality used to be the name of the game. There was a blanket ban on going to the cinema, whimsical purchases of steel utensils and other goodies. In hindsight, I realize that such trying times have taught me a lot about controlling my desires and greed.

Thankfully, being in a fairly high position, Mava didn't take too long to return the money he'd borrowed. In about three months, he returned the entire sum in one stroke. That very day, Appa paid off the remaining interest and brought home the gold. When Appa gave Amma her jewellery, both of them cried. Akka and I were also in tears. Amma placed those jewels before the idols in the pooja room and lit the ghee lamp. We all prostrated before God. With his own hands, Appa delicately slid the bangles on Amma's hands and placed the chain around her neck. After that, they never took out any loans in their lives. They just didn't have the courage to borrow.

Having seen such hardship, could Amma have let me take out a loan? She was acting purely on her love and concern. Obviously, she'd never wish to cause me any loss, would she? But back then, I wasn't mature enough to understand that.

The virtue called empathy is seldom found in the youth, bubbling with health. For a woman who opposed taking out a loan so strongly, didn't Amma surprise me with her mature and rational views on Vastu? She wasn't gullible enough to believe that adverse Vastu could harm her son in any way. While I always kept blaming Amma for the BTM Layout plot fiasco, I never admired her mature rationality with regard to Vastu at all.

One often hears the high-sounding phrase 'life values'. But if someone suddenly asks for its definition, we struggle to define it properly. I've tried to assess my life values based on this particular event in my life. While Amma caused me some loss due to her foolishness, she also stopped me from getting into debt only out of her love and concern for my well-being. Another value I have since understood and drawn solace from was that I was probably not destined to own that particular plot of land. Eventually, it all boils down to our individual personalities. The fact of the matter is, if we overlook the element of love and cling only to pointless logic, our values tend to fall apart. All our thoughts should at least have an undercurrent of empathy, if not compassion.

Empathy is about getting into the skin of the other person and deeply connecting with their thoughts, feelings and experiences. Empathizing isn't easy. One has to work hard to attain this ability. Once we become empathetic, we can clearly understand the pains and pleasures of other people, and the reasons behind their decisions. If one develops this skill, one will never be cruel to anyone else. Most crimes in today's world would never happen if we all practised more empathy. In fact, empathy is the key to world peace. But it's hard to teach it. Nevertheless, while it can't be taught, it can definitely be caught. One has to cultivate empathy, and once it becomes part of our nature almost instantaneously the world becomes a beautiful place.

Recently I reread the late Tarasu's famous novel, *Hamsa Geethe*. I was so impressed by how Tarasu explained empathy in it. Placing two tuned tambouras in two corners of a silent room without any breeze, if we strum just one of the tambouras, the other one will start resonating by itself. In a way, aren't we all living tambouras too? Isn't it humane to resonate the vibes of a fellow human? But is it so easy in a world full of clutter? No, not at all. That's the cause of all our irritations, jealousy, anger, restlessness, hostility and whatnot!

22

THE TEETOTALLER

2 March 2015

'WHAT? DON'T TELL ME YOU DON'T DRINK alcohol at all!' He sounded genuinely surprised. He was at least ten years younger to me.

'No, sir, I've never tried it,' I confessed.

'But why! Any health issues?'

'Nothing of that sort. I never felt a need for it. As none of my close buddies in college consumed alcohol, I also stayed away. Sorry, I'm a teetotaller,' I replied with a smile.

'In fact, I'm the one who should be sorry for you, dude. But then, such things do happen, you know. If one isn't lucky enough to get a good peer group in college, life is bound to get a bit boring in the later years. But don't you worry, dude. Whoever said opportunity knocks only once was talking bullshit. One can always catch up with the things you missed out on in college. It's never too late to develop a new pastime, you know?'

I didn't know what to say—he sounded sympathetic enough to my 'condition'. Sensing that I wasn't keen on heeding his advice, he thoughtfully sipped his drink and slowly moved to another table in search of better company. Staring at my boring fruit punch, I slipped deep into thought.

All my good friends in college typically hailed from middle-class or lower-middle class families. Only the nerds and studious kids made it to our prestigious institute. Almost all of my friends had availed education loans from banks to study here. Only a few boys received an allowance from their homes. The rest had to manage our monthly expenses from the bank loan. Naturally, we used to be very measured in our expenditure. I'd even say that we were quite stingy. We strictly avoided eating out. In our final year we mustered up a little courage and dared to have the occasional masala dosa or ice cream—however, we'd feel guilty about it for days on end. In such dire straits, we obviously couldn't afford to squander money on luxuries like liquor.

Of course, the hostel had a few rich kids as well. They were as good as anybody else in academics. We often interacted with them freely about our studies and other academic activities. However, our camaraderie never extended beyond academic interactions. They'd often go out to party hard and return rather late at night. Within two weeks of landing at the institute, they'd discovered all the good pubs and bars in the city. But none in my closest circle ever dared to enter that world of indulgence. The undefined gulf between the privileged and the not-so-privileged remained until our graduation.

As I said earlier, all my friends were quite serious about their studies. Everybody was very hardworking and committed. Maybe having witnessed poverty or for the sake of helping our parents, all of us used to score well in exams. I'd invariably get a high rank every semester. It obviously helped all of us secure good campus placements as well. I must admit that the sudden influx of cash we saw once we started receiving monthly salaries left us quite dazed.

Amma loved to brag about my accomplishments to anyone who would listen. 'My son is so lucky indeed. All his friends and classmates are such a good lot. No vices of any kind. No smoking, no drinking … no gambling! I should be really grateful to God for all his blessings. Otherwise, not everybody is fortunate to have such good company,' she'd say.

Now, here I was at this party, with someone telling me that if one isn't lucky enough to find a good peer group while in college, life is bound to get a bit boring in the later years!

How stupidly I got carried away by his words and started introspecting! Indeed the times change, and rather drastically at that.

I'm aware that not everyone who comes from my kind of background lives like me. I know of several people who can't sleep unless they have had a couple of pegs. Then there are those who call themselves social drinkers, the ones who drink occasionally. These guys trust alcohol to spice up celebrations, such as birthdays, anniversaries or friendly get-togethers. They have almost come to believe that one cannot have a good time without liquor. After all these years, only a few of my old friends have remained teetotallers like me. But this small ilk doesn't seem to be sure if it should be proud or ashamed!

As a child, I hadn't seen any of my family members, or even close relatives, smoke or drink. I was brought up in an environment that regarded all vices as deadly sins. This feeling was so deeply ingrained in me that I used to be wary of smokers and drinkers. The fathers of most of my school friends were alcoholics. I'd dread going to their houses after dusk for fear of what I'd witness there.

However, such notions disappeared after I joined college. Many of my rich friends used to consume alcohol on weekends and on holidays. As opposed to what I'd presumed, they were all very smart, responsible and large-hearted. Even while drinking, they'd crack jokes and chat with everyone very jovially. The next day, they'd be totally focused on their studies like always. However, despite my changing attitude to the 'sin' that this vice carried, I could never gather the courage to try it out myself. Moreover, I wasn't inclined to spend my hard-earned money on something so trivial. Maybe I was influenced by my circle of intimate friends, who were also teetotallers like me. And so I never crossed the Lakshman Rekha.

Somewhere deep down, I still secretly nursed a holier-than-thou attitude. I'd pride myself on thinking that I would never stray easily in life. I'd sometimes think that my friends with such vices would someday fall sick with some deadly disease and regret their mistakes. Luckily, such stupid arrogance got decimated over time.

After I joined the corporate world, I had to adjust to its culture. Most companies just needed an excuse to throw a party with free-flowing alcohol. I found it hard to adapt to this new milieu. I'd often sit alone in an obscure corner, sipping a soft drink, while my colleagues around me got more and more boisterous. I didn't want to come across as a snob by avoiding such parties. But by staying aloof in a rejoicing crowd, I started developing a complex. While my colleagues eagerly awaited these parties, the very thought of it made me feel sick.

I wasn't the only teetotaller in our company. There were a few hyper-religious guys—the kind who put a long, conspicuous tilak on their foreheads, fasted on Ekadashi, believed overseas travel to be a sin and kept seeking the cancellation of international assignments. But I just couldn't gel with such extreme views. On the other hand, my upbringing didn't let me indulge in some casual, light drinking either. In short, I had a drinking problem—but of a different kind.

Many of my colleagues used to say that climbing up the corporate ladder would be harder for teetotallers. Everyone seemed to believe that a glass of liquor in hand could be a great icebreaker while dealing with international clients. Many vowed that a single party could accomplish more than a series of meetings ever could. It may sound a little far-fetched, but I've even heard that some companies conduct their interviews in pubs in order to get a proper assessment of the potential of a prospective employee.

Initially, I'd get really disturbed by such talks. But after working in the corporate sector for over two decades, I've realized that such beliefs are just rubbish. Corporates always value an employee who earnestly puts his heart and soul into his work. All that foreign clients are interested in is our commitment to meticulously completing a project and delivering it on time. They really don't care whether you drink or not. A good, reliable employee is all they expect. True, going out for drinks with your superiors may help in opening certain doors when it comes to sales and marketing. Having said that, over the years, I've seen many teetotallers achieve phenomenal success in marketing as well.

There's one more popular myth about drinking. I've heard some people argue that it's impossible to weather the cold of certain countries without any alcohol. But from my personal experience of having lived in several countries, I can vouch that it's far from true. Just a couple more blankets and woollen clothes are more than enough to survive in cold countries. If one is lucky, one can perhaps enjoy the luxury of hugging the warm body of a partner as well.

In fact, I have had no problems living in extremely cold conditions without a single drop of alcohol. In most foreign countries, people respect the personal choices of individuals and no one is ever ridiculed for one's choices. Unlike in India, I have never had to sit in isolation with my soft drink when I am abroad.

I must admit that there have been times when I have felt inferior to my friends and colleagues because I don't drink. After working in the corporate world for about two decades, I entered the world of literature. The literary world is so drenched in alcohol that the guys who *don't* drink are considered sinners here. Here, it's immaterial if a litterateur has written any good literature or not. But the one who doesn't drink tends to easily fall out of literary circles.

In the contemporary literary world, a young writer who is yet to produce even a few lines of quality literature can be found already sloshed at literary meets and fests. While participating in upcountry literature festivals and workshops, if I feel bored in the company of drunk writers and poets, my only option is to loaf around an unfamiliar city with my solitude as companion. Sometimes, being lonely in a crowd could be really frustrating.

In a section of the literary circle, it is believed that smoking and drinking provide inspiration for the creation of good literature. Liquor is regarded as a panacea and something that paves the way for good oration. Hence, a few people even consider drinking and smoking as occupational necessities of being a writer. But again, we get ample examples to disprove such misgivings in our Kannada literary world itself. It's a fact that nobody has been able to produce great literature only because of alcohol. At the same time, nobody has produced bad literature due to the absence of alcohol either. The quality of literature is purely a matter of the competence of its writer.

It is not easy to digest being alienated from a group. It calls for a special conviction to hold out against such repudiation. For whatever reason, I couldn't cultivate the habit of drinking. I don't see any prospect of doing so in the future either. I don't regret having missed out on something extraordinary.

At the same time, I don't gloat as though not drinking alcohol is a huge achievement in itself. This is just who I am. It's my prerogative to choose my likes and dislikes. I have the right to live my life the way I want to. Just as we choose the kinds of books we read, the type of food we eat, whether to drink alcohol or not is also a personal choice. No one has the right to object to that choice. But it's quite embarrassing that we are living in a time when we are required to defend ourselves even in such personal matters!

Perhaps that's why when someone asks me, 'What, don't you drink?' I've developed the brazenness to counter them by asking, 'Of course not, is there a problem?'

In a way, it has become my self-defence as well.

23

GRADUATION DAYS

22 February 2023

WHEN I WAS DOING MY PRE-UNIVERSITY COURSE (PUC), it never crossed Appa's mind that I could join an engineering college and become an engineer. It never crossed mine either. Coming from a lower middle-class family, we kept our dreams affordable. Those days, Appa's entire salary was not exceeding four-digits, and his pension was another two hundred rupees.

As Appa was quite old by the time Akka and I were born, in order to fulfil his responsibilities towards us, he worked even after retirement. His income was just about enough for our monthly groceries bill and the instalments we had to pay to the textile showroom, from where we bought new clothes for Ugadi or Deepavali.

Obviously, an expensive degree like engineering was never on the cards. Under such circumstances, Appa conveniently admitted me to a BSc programme in a local government-run college in our town. He also enrolled me in a typewriting course when I was doing my PUC. Initially, he was a bit reluctant when I insisted that I'd only learn

Kannada typing. However, after his friends assured him that in the coming days, governments would be giving priority to Kannada, he agreed. I passed junior typing in my first year of PUC. In the second year, when I completed the senior typing exam with first-class marks, Appa happily said, 'Well done, putta. Now you can easily get into the government service as a clerk.'

Meanwhile, all my friends decided to go to Bellary to write the newly introduced engineering entrance test, CET. My family could afford the bus fare to Bellary. As I could stay in a relative's house, there was no need to worry about boarding and lodging expenses either. So when I asked Appa if I could go with my friends and write the exam, he didn't decline. As I had been pestering Appa to take me somewhere after my PU exams, he thought he was hitting two birds with a single stone by sending me to Bellary.

'Don't forget to carry your hall ticket to the exam,' Appa reiterated multiple times.

Amma kept telling me, 'Don't forget to do Sandhyavandane.'

After finishing the exam, I stayed on for two extra days in Bellary and then returned home. In about a week, I forgot all about the CET and got busy with my BSc degree at the local college.

Suddenly, one day, we came to know that the CET results had been announced. Those days, they used to stick the result sheet only on the notice board of Bellary Medical College. People in our town got to know about the results only after a couple of days. Appa didn't see any point in wasting more money on the bus fare merely to see the results. I gave my hall ticket number to my friends and requested them to check my ranking as well. They told me that my ranking was a hundred-odd. The next best ranking in our town, obtained by one of my friends, was three thousand–plus. But my lecturers found my ranking unbelievable. Even the principal of my college felt that it was too good to be true. In fact, I wasn't sure if I had done so well myself.

The principal met Appa and told him, 'No doubt your son is one of our best, but his rank appears to be a little far-fetched. What if they have missed one or two digits while printing out the results? I suggest you confirm it yourself before you share the good news with others. You shouldn't unnecessarily become the laughing stock, you know?'

As per the principal's suggestion, we kept quiet for a few days. Meanwhile, I continued my BSc. Finally, Appa sent me to Bellary to see my results for myself. I quite nervously enquired with the authorities, who reassured me that my hundred-plus rank was indeed true. I returned home, flooded with a sense of relief.

My outstanding performance in CET suddenly disrupted Appa's plans for me. While people praising me with envy wherever he went made him gloat with pride, he'd get scared when he heard them speak about the hefty fees that engineering colleges charged. As we didn't have any relatives or friends who had a degree in engineering, we had no clear idea about how anything worked.

Meanwhile, a senior officer in Appa's office asked us to visit. Incidentally, the officer's son was my classmate in college. His rank was some five thousand–plus. Perhaps his father was a bit upset about it. Although the officer appreciated my performance, he scared Appa by adding, 'Are you aware that you'll have to shell out at least twenty-five thousand bucks in four years? How will you manage it?'

Seemingly petrified, Appa mumbled, 'No idea what to do, sir.'

With a smirk on his face, the officer advised Appa, 'You just listen to me and don't get carried away by your son's rank. Wise men don't bite off more than they can chew. Don't be too greedy and aspire for things beyond your means. Let him do his graduation for free at the local degree college. If he's lucky, he'll surely get a clerk's job somewhere.'

Visibly upset, Appa wiped the sweat off his forehead with his handkerchief. The officer gave us sweets to celebrate his son's CET performance before we left. As we walked back, although our tongues tasted sweet, we felt bitter inside.

Appa finally choked out, 'Let's not venture into the impossible, putta. You just do your BSc here itself.'

I readily agreed. In our small town, there were not many who could properly guide us at such crucial junctures.

But I was fortunate.

Halfway through our journey home, we ran into Gopanna Master, who was my teacher in school. He congratulated me and Appa, and said, 'I'm so glad that your son brought a good name not only to our school but to our entire town. Put him into some good engineering college, so that his life will be set.'

Appa got teary-eyed and shared his financial woes with Gopanna Master.

'Fortunately, there's no need to worry about such things anymore,' he told Appa. 'I've heard that nowadays banks provide education loans at reasonable interest rates. If the boy joins a good college and studies well, he can earn a lot of money going forward. It won't be a problem for him to pay off the loan in instalments. Such opportunities don't knock twice. Don't worry! God is there, he'll take care of you.'

Taking leave from Gopanna Master, as we resumed our walk homeward, Appa asked, 'Can you stay away from home, all alone in a hostel, and pursue your studies?'

Appa's words sounded like music to my ears. I nodded my head and said, 'Yes, of course.'

However, Appa didn't really like the idea of burdening my young shoulders with an education loan. So, although he decided to let me apply to an engineering college, he deferred applying for a loan for the time being.

I got a seat in the prestigious Regional Engineering College, Surathkal, now known as National Institute of Technology Karnataka. Although Surathkal was quite far away from my hometown, everyone said that the college was very good and only the best got a seat there. I packed my things into a military trunk and a bag.

Carrying all my baggage and a rolled bed, I boarded the bus to Bellary. I would then transfer to another bus that would take me to Surathkal.

Shoving a few pairs of yajnopavita and a set of panchapatra-uddharane into my luggage, Amma said, 'Don't forget to do your Sandhyavandane at least twice a day.'

I nodded my head.

Meanwhile, Akka touched my heart with her special parting gift. Tearing off the empty sheets from my PU notebooks and collecting the leftover sheets from her own notebooks, she'd stitched three notebooks with thick wrappers. Just as I was about to leave, she surprised me by giving me three hand-stitched notebooks with my name written boldly in red ink.

Although Appa wanted to come to Surathkal to drop me off, we simply couldn't afford the bus fare and he had to stay back. Just before I boarded the bus, Appa took me aside and gave me two hundred rupees. But this unexpected extra cash suddenly made me very tense. I spent the entire journey worrying about protecting it from getting stolen.

Somewhere in his autobiography, Gandhiji speaks about Nirbal ke Bal Ram. His pious mind firmly believed that Lord Ram empowers all the powerless. I truly believe in this too. All my financial problems vanished miraculously. My college was a government institution. Yet, we had to pay four hundred rupees as fees every semester. When I was just about joining, a new scheme was introduced. The institute conducted an examination based on our PU syllabus. Students passing that exam would not only get their fee exempted but would also receive a hundred-rupee scholarship every semester. As I easily cleared that exam, I never had to pay any fees.

But the monthly mess bill would still come to around one hundred and fifty rupees. In addition, my other maintenance expenses would be about fifty to hundred rupees. Sending two hundred and fifty rupees to cover these costs was beyond Appa's means. But Nirbal ke Ram didn't let me down.

Those days, 'ragging' was common in my institute. The college's culture demanded that us freshers do everything the seniors demanded of us. We juniors would do our best to impress the seniors by being their dutiful sidekicks. While it mitigated the ragging intensity to an extent, we had to endure the rest helplessly. However, after the first month everybody becomes friends. Although ragging tends to turn ugly occasionally, mostly the seniors use this as an ice-breaker of sorts. Generally, they'd be curious to know about our family background, financial status, PU scores, CET ranking, etc.

During this time, a senior began asking me questions about my background. He extensively enquired about my family members, Appa's salary, my expenses and how we planned to meet them, and so on. Later, he told me that a company owned by a Jain family in Bangalore was providing financial assistance to studious and needy students, and suggested that I apply for it. He told me that he also came from a modest background and was a recipient of the assistance extended by the company.

'I am not a Jain,' I confessed to him.

'Neither am I. You don't have to be. It's not caste or religion based. One has to be needy and deserving, that's all they look for. You just try. Let's see what happens.' He also took the initiative of writing a request letter to the company and procured the required application form. Together, we completed the application and sent it to the company's Bangalore address.

In about a fortnight, I received a reply. It said that, every month, the company would pay me a sum of four hundred rupees towards my expenses. They assured me that the scholarship would be paid even during vacations. Their only condition was that the scholarship would be paid only if I scored over seventy per cent in every semester. I just couldn't believe it.

When I wrote about it to Appa, he wrote back saying, 'Even I find it hard to believe. These days, there are cheaters everywhere. In any case, you should be on your guard. We have to be careful all the time. Who knows who's up to what?'

I didn't know exactly what I had to do in order to stay on guard and be more careful. Unable to figure out what Appa meant, I grew anxious. At no point in time would I have more than fifty bucks on me. So, even if someone fleeced me, they would hardly get anything. But that's typical middle-class apprehension for you. So, although I didn't know what it really meant to be 'on guard', I decided to be more careful! But all my fears dissolved when I received a single cheque for two thousand and four hundred rupees from the company. At four hundred rupees a month, my first semester of college was now covered. I had never seen so much money in my life. As I held the cheque in my hands, I noticed that I was shivering slightly.

The company stood by their promise all through the four years of my engineering. I also scored over seventy per cent in every semester and sent them copies of my marks as proof. I never met anyone from their company ever. But my hostel warden told me that they were keeping a tab on my conduct on the campus, and that, once in a while, they got a brief about my attendance and general demeanour from the college management. But they never tried to meet me in person.

Although the scholarship covered my expenses entirely, Appa still felt it was his duty to send me some money. So, every other month, he'd send me some. But I had no need for it. Maybe my humble background didn't allow me to spend money freely. Mangalore city was just eight to ten kilometres away from our campus. Some of my wealthier friends would visit Mangalore at least a couple of times a month and party hard. I never dared to do such things—I'd often worry what would happen if I ever strayed from the path of righteousness and Appa–Amma or the Jain company found out! In the first three years of my college, I'd never gone to Mangalore spending my own money. I never felt like spending a rupee more than what was absolutely necessary. But after every semester, I had to go to Mangalore to board the bus to Bellary.

On those days, I'd make an exception to my frugality. After finishing my lunch in the hostel, I'd put on my backpack and leave for Mangalore in the afternoon. There, I'd roam around the city and have dinner in a good restaurant. After dinner, I'd pamper myself with a large cup of Ideal ice-cream before boarding the night bus to Bellary. However, sitting in the bus, I'd invariably feel guilty about my lavish indulgence.

Thanks to my frugality, by the time I finished engineering, I had nearly three thousand rupees in my bank account. I thought of gifting something to Amma with that money. Those days, we didn't have a gas stove at home. Amma would cook in a hearth, using firewood. If the firewood happened to be damp, Amma's eyes would turn red from all the smoke. Moreover, I was quite disturbed by a mishap that had taken place at home a couple of years before.

Our kitchen was rather small. Within that tiny kitchen, we had a tiny pooja corner, a little washing sink and a manual stone grinder. Amma did all her grinding and pounding chores right there with that grinding stone. Although she did all the cooking in the firewood hearth, she used a coal oven to prepare any offerings for God. As she meticulously observed all the do's and don'ts of a traditional Madhwa household, she placed the consecrated coal oven a little away from the firewood hearth. Amma's cooking chores and pooja rituals would go on side by side in our congested kitchen.

On that fateful day, after offering pooja and taking out an aarthi to the gods, in a hurry to resume cooking, Amma, without paying any heed, sat down on the coal oven filled with hot embers by mistakes. She suffered serious burns and her deep wounds took several months to heal. We were all worried because Amma was diabetic. Fortunately, all the wounds eventually healed completely.

From the money I'd saved from my scholarship, I got a mixer and a gas stove for Amma. With the arrival of the new goodies, there was a festive ambience in the house. A few neighbours dropped in to join the inauguration ceremony, as it was the first gas stove in our entire lane. Amma applied kumkuma to the mixer and the gas stove, and decorated them with hand-twisted cotton garlands called gejje vastras. She then took out an aarthi to welcome the new appliances home. Friendly neighbours rejoiced and joined us in the celebration. A few obtained Amma's permission and my approval to grind their dough in our new mixer. Amma served everyone a spoonful of sugar in their palms, and called it sweet distribution. The whole lane seemed to be celebrating the slight upliftment in the lifestyle of one of their own.

Sitting on cloud nine, Amma generously granted me a big concession. Although I had carried the panchapatra-uddharane with me to the hostel, I'd never done the Sandhyavandane. The typical vulgar talk of foul-mouthed teenagers, posters of naked models and actresses on all the walls, frequent titillating chats and erotic discussions, and the stench of ill-maintained toilets—nothing in my hostel was conducive to doing Sandhyavandane.

From my conduct and mannerisms, Amma would somehow come to know that I wasn't doing Sandhyavandane in the hostel and would grumble about it restlessly. But surprisingly, after I bought her the mixer and the stove, her grumbling stopped for good. With that concession, the ritual of Sandhyavandane fell out of my routine completely.

Thanks to my good performance in the campus interview and consistent high scores, I got a good placement in the beginning of my final year. The salary was at least three to four times higher than Appa's salary. Appa found it too absurd to believe. No one in my family had ever heard of anyone getting a job even before getting their degree. Landing a high-paying job almost a whole year before completing the course was too good to be true. Several ominous doubts cropped up in Appa's mind: Why would anyone pay such a high salary to a rookie? Does the job involve any anti-national or criminal activities? Was I being baited by corporate scamsters?

Appa's natural love for me conflicted with the countless apprehensions in his mind. But some of his friends assured him that he didn't have to worry. I also tried to convince him by quoting several examples of my seniors who had got good placements. By that time, Appa's salary had just crossed four digits. I sensed the steep disparity in our salaries even kindling a spark of jealousy in Appa. 'Newly passed-out kids shouldn't be paid absurd amounts of money. It's not a good trend,' he declared.

I was pleasantly amused by Appa's unfounded apprehensions. By then, I'd grown taller than Appa. Putting my arm around his shoulders, I whispered, 'Don't worry, Appa, nothing untoward is going to happen.'

Once I started working, my family never had to flirt with poverty again. I kept getting offered better, more high-paying jobs from time to time. Appa–Amma started getting more respect at the grocery store and the textile showroom. The whole neighbourhood started looking at them with awe. As Appa wanted to keep himself engaged, he continued to work for a few more years. Eventually, when they moved to Bangalore to stay with me, he finally retired.

Slowly, to an extent, I got used to the idea that one didn't really have to get so worked up to spend money a little generously. But Appa–Amma couldn't change their ways. Whenever we ate out or bought some new clothes or goodies, they'd calculate the expenses and get frightened. I'd just smile at them.

The story of my graduation days is not all that important when it's viewed just as a story of an individual. But as a story of millions of Indian students of my time, it assumes significance. It has been thirty-five years since I graduated from college. The sums of money we struggled to arrange in my youth and which felt substantial then seem like a pittance now. But I know how hard we had to toil to earn that kind of money back then. We'd think a dozen times before spending five paise.

Amid all that hardship, the day I gifted the mixer and the stove to Amma has been deeply etched in my mind. Every time I remember that day, a sense of happiness washes over me. For thousands of lower-middle-class families, a mixer or a gas stove symbolizes their success. These successes can be viewed in so many other things—the small rural school that enabled one of its students to get a spot in a prestigious institution of national repute; the college that provided a poor student like me quality education nearly for free.

On the whole, I view it as the success of our great nation. If such springs of joy keep spurting in the families dwelling in our remote hamlets from time to time, we can rest assured that the country is on its path to progress. I feel these little developments reflect the state of our country much better than the multiple metrics devised by expert economists.

There was one thing that haunted me for a long time—Appa's envy at my first salary. Although I initially thought it was funny, over time, it kept raising various questions in my mind. Appa soon forgot about it and was busy bragging about his son's achievements to anyone who would listen. But in my mind, this incident felt like a symbol of the changes taking place in our country. India opened up its economy in the early 1990s. Perhaps Appa's jealousy was a reflection of that liberalization. Brooding over it gave me many insights.

Ten years later, those insights inspired me to write a short story titled 'Ugadi'. Exploring the gulf between two generations, or eras, I delved into the dynamics of the aggression of the new and the unrest of the old, and narrated the pain and suffering resulting from such conflicts. 'Ugadi' was well received by readers, and it was included as the main story in one of my anthologies with the same title. I'm glad that 'Ugadi' has now been included in the curriculum of many undergraduate and postgraduate courses.

Two years ago, Vishweswaraya Technical University, widely known as VTU, introduced Kannada as a compulsory subject for all their first-semester engineering students. Luckily for me, the experts chose to include 'Ugadi' in its syllabus. I feel so proud that all the engineering students of VTU are reading my story now. If my story can inspire students to set out and achieve goals that can make their dad envious, I'd be more than satisfied about my writing career.

There's another important thing that I must share with you. Although it's self-deprecating, it would be unfair to hide it. I told you that a Jain company had funded my four years of engineering, right? After I got my first job, I wrote to them sharing the good news and thanked them for supporting me when I needed it the most.

As I had provided my new address in my letter, they sent me a reply. After congratulating me on getting a lucrative job, they'd added, 'As you are getting a good salary now, can you please consider returning the scholarship money we'd paid you?'

I cursed myself for writing to them unnecessarily. Perhaps years of poverty had made me so miserly and mean that I couldn't bear the thought of suddenly parting with so much money in one go.

I never replied to them.

They also didn't follow up on the matter any further. Had they been a little more assertive, I'd probably have returned the money out of fear. But they never did anything of that sort.

In about a decade, the sway that money held over me waned. I gradually started helping a number of needy students myself. I donated many times more than what I had received. But the fact that I didn't return my scholarship money to that company still pinches on my conscience.

Maybe generosity takes a while to set in. Perhaps a person just stepping out of poverty can't be large-hearted instantaneously. Maturity and a charitable disposition require a fair amount of seasoning, I suppose. Time alone can achieve it.

ABOUT THE AUTHOR

Vasudhendra is a Kannada author whose primary forms of expression include novels, short stories, and personal essays. Recognized as the first queer writer in Kannada literature, he is based in Bengaluru. He founded the publishing house Chanda Pustaka and, for over two decades, has been identifying and publishing new voices in Kannada literature.

Among his numerous books are the critically acclaimed *Mohanaswamy* (HarperCollins India, 2019), which has been translated into several languages; the widely popular historical novel *Tejo Tungabhadra: Tributaries of Time* (Penguin Random House India, 2022); and *Unforgiving City and Other Stories* (Penguin Random House India, 2021).

ABOUT THE TRANSLATOR

Narayan Shankaran has served as a development officer with the Life Insurance Corporation of India for over three decades. Holding an MBA and a PhD in management studies with a specialization in emotional and social intelligence, he is an accomplished writer and translator between Kannada and English. His original English essay collection, *Figuratively Speaking - Musings of the Lockdown* (2020), complements his distinguished translations, including S.V. Ranganath's Kannada travelogue *Sindhu Darshan* (English edition, 2019); Guruprasad Kaginele's short stories, published as *The Preferred Pronoun and Other Stories* (2024); and, recently, Kaginele's critically acclaimed Kannada novel *KAAYAA* (Penguin Random House India, 2025).

HarperCollins *Publishers* India

At HarperCollins India, we believe in telling the best stories and finding the widest readership for our books in every format possible. We started publishing in 1992; a great deal has changed since then, but what has remained constant is the passion with which our authors write their books, the love with which readers receive them, and the sheer joy and excitement that we as publishers feel in being a part of the publishing process.

Over the years, we've had the pleasure of publishing some of the finest writing from the subcontinent and around the world, including several award-winning titles and some of the biggest bestsellers in India's publishing history. But nothing has meant more to us than the fact that millions of people have read the books we published, and that somewhere, a book of ours might have made a difference.

As we look to the future, we go back to that one word—a word which has been a driving force for us all these years.

Read.

Harper Collins · Harper Sport · HARPER FICTION · HARPER NON-FICTION · हार्पर हिन्दी

HARPER LEARNING · HARPER VANTAGE · HCCB HARPERCOLLINS CHILDREN'S BOOKS · 4th · HARPER PERENNIAL

HARPER DESIGN · BOOKTOPUS · HARPER BUSINESS